Understanding Sensory Dysfunction

Understanding Sensory Dysfunction

Learning, Development and Sensory Dysfunction in Autism Spectrum Disorders, ADHD, Learning Disabilities and Bipolar Disorder

Polly Godwin Emmons and
Liz McKendry Anderson

Jessica Kingsley Publishers
London and Philadelphia

Diagnostic criteria for pervasive developmental disorder not otherwise specified, autistic disorder and Asperger's disorder on pages 69–72 reprinted with permission from the *Diagnostic and Statistical Manual of Mental Disorders, Fourth Edition*, Copyright © 2000. American Psychiatric Association.

First published in 2005
by Jessica Kingsley Publishers
116 Pentonville Road
London N1 9JB, UK
and
400 Market Street, Suite 400
Philadelphia, PA 19106, USA

www.jkp.com

Copyright © Polly Godwin Emmons and Liz McKendry Anderson 2005
Second impression 2005
Third impression 2006

Library of Congress Cataloging in Publication Data

Emmons, Polly Godwin, 1960-
    Understanding sensory dysfunction : learning, development and sensory dysfunction in autism spectrum disorders, ADHD, learning disabilities and bipolar disorder / Polly Godwin Emmons and Liz McKendry Anderson.
        p. cm.
    Includes bibliographical references and index.
    ISBN-13: 978-1-84310-806-1 (pbk.)
    ISBN-10: 1-84310-806-2 (pbk.)
    1. Sensory integration dysfunction in children. 2. Developmentally disabled children. 3. Learning disabled children. 4. Autism in children. 5. Attention-deficit hyperactivity disorder. 6. Manic-depressive illness in children. I. Anderson, Liz McKendry, 1961- II. Title.
    RJ496.S44E465 2005
    618.92'8588--dc22

                                        2005005923

British Library Cataloguing in Publication Data
A CIP catalogue record for this book is available from the British Library

ISBN-13: 978 1 84310 806 1
ISBN-10: 1 84310 806 2

Printed and Bound in Great Britain by
Athenaeum Press, Gateshead, Tyne and Wear

To Laura, a daughter to treasure and a wonderful sister.
To Dylan, a son to cherish and a devoted brother.

Polly

To Richard, for his continued support of all of my endeavors.
To Lindy, Ellie, Julia, and Carter, who bring me my greatest joys.

Liz

Acknowledgements

We thank our families and friends who have been listeners and supporters throughout this project. A special thank you to Eileen, who cared enough about our children, and our families, to throw us a lifeline when we most needed it; and who encourages us to continue to see the possibilities.

Contents

Introduction   9
    What we would like the reader to take away from this book   11
    The ultimate goal   12

1.   What is Sensory Integration?   14
    A brief history of sensory integration   14
    Sensory processing   16
    The sensory systems   19
    The developmental timeline   20
    Social and emotional development and sensory integration   28
    Development as viewed through a sensory lens   29

2.   What is Sensory Dysfunction?   32
    Signs and symptoms   32
    Dysfunction in the sensory systems   34
    Logan's day   36
    Sensory dysfunction through the developmental stages   41
    The functional areas as viewed through a sensory lens   50
    Assessment and evaluation   55
    Programs and services   64

3.   Concomitant Diagnoses   67
    What is an autism spectrum disorder?   69
    What are learning disabilities?   72
    What is ADHD?   73
    What is bipolar disorder?   74
    To medicate or not to medicate…this is the question   75

4.   Sensory Dysfunction at School   76
    Everyone has a job to do   76
    What special education is, and is not   77
    The "players" on a child's team   78
    Analyzing possible sensory dysfunction and offering solutions 80
    The teacher as detective   86
    Home/school partnerships   99
    Adapting to the child   101

5.   At Home and at School: Looking at Strategies   116
    Management techniques   116
    Considering and modifying the environment   122
    Self-care strategies   127

6. More About Asperger's Syndrome   130
    Diagnosing Asperger's from the DSM-IV: Selecting from the menu   *131*
    Social and communication deficits: Pragmatics made easy   *138*
    Colin's day   *147*

7. Ellie and Dylan: Ten Years Later   151
    Introduction   *151*
    Ellie's story (part one)   *151*
    Ellie's story (part two)   *154*
    Dylan's story (part one)   *156*
    Dylan's story (part two)   *159*

    In Conclusion   164

    APPENDIX 1: SENSORY INTEGRATION ACTIVITIES   165

    APPENDIX 2: TREATMENT OPTIONS   169

    APPENDIX 3: RESOURCES   171

    INDEX   172

Introduction

A decade has passed since we first felt compelled to share our stories as mothers of children with sensory dysfunction. Now the feeling has gripped us once again to continue the story and advocate for the children with sensory processing difficulties, for the parents, for the teachers. As the years have passed, we find ourselves evolving both personally and professionally. In 1995, when we were writing *Unlocking the Mysteries of Sensory Dysfunction* (Anderson and Emmons 1996), we wrote from the perspective of parents of young children with significant sensory issues, and we were struggling to keep our heads above water. These were supposed to be the salad days—while the best was yet to come. However, the dream did not always match the reality. When our paths crossed, we instinctively realized that our individual struggles and the challenges our children presented were perhaps reflective of a common issue...sensory dysfunction.

In *Unlocking the Mysteries of Sensory Dysfunction*, we shared our early journey into a world where there was very little information (thank goodness for A. Jean Ayres and her book *Sensory Integration and the Child* (1979)) about children with sensory issues. We then began to consider the relationship between sensory dysfunction and other diagnoses such as ADHD, learning disabilities, autism spectrum disorders, psychiatric disorders, cerebral palsy, Down syndrome...the list goes on and on. We were aware that sometimes the sensory issues were the "big" piece and other times they were the "small" piece or were negligible. We had to face the facts that while we had very different children and very different lifestyles, the commonalities were simply too powerful to be attributed to chance. It started off as two moms talking in a waiting room while our children received early intervention services, sharing our experiences, and beginning to search for more information. It then became our mission to become more informed and more actively involved. We both called everyone we knew; we still came up with very few resources. We read all of the clinical/medical "stuff" on sensory dysfunction (with dictionary in hand) and started calling authors and others considered experts. Once we gathered as much information as we could find, we began to translate this information in terms of our own lives, what seemed applicable and appeared to have the most relevance. We did this because we felt we needed to help our children, ourselves, and our families, and ultimately to help and support other children with sensory issues and their families. The "collection of symptoms" we were seeing in our children was simply not going away. Rather, it was morphing and changing, but certainly not just going away. This was true for our children and other children as well. This was a life-altering realization! Our subsequent work in homes, schools, and community organizations only serves to validate and reaffirm this commitment.

In retrospect, it is those early experiences and struggles that continue to define and sculpt who we are both personally and professionally as mothers and as teachers. Back in 1992, we had few role models or real direction as to where we were going and what we should do for our children with sensory dysfunction. At that point in our lives, whether or not to have our children evaluated, the evaluation process itself, the need for and access to services, and just everyday family life were often overwhelming. Yet these early experiences were a great motivator that ultimately prompted us to go with our "gut" feelings, continue to seek information and objectively to begin to document what we were seeing in our own children. It was in fact their sensory dysfunction that ultimately drove us to seek further evaluations... Dylan was diagnosed in 1995 with Asperger's syndrome. Ellie's evaluation in 1996 was "highly suggestive of PDD-NOS", and in 2002 she was diagnosed with ADHD and mood disorder. In addition, Liz's son, Carter, was diagnosed with central auditory processing disorder, ADHD and multiple learning disabilities in 2001. For Dylan, Ellie, and Carter, as with many children, their sensory dysfunction continues to be at the very core of who they are and how they respond to the world around them.

As we began to observe and document Ellie and Dylan's behaviors, back in the early 1990s, we started becoming aware of patterns of behavior in children (and adults!), and began to seek out other parents who had similar concerns about their children, attempting to fit the pieces together.

What we would like the reader to take away from this book

We have been the parents of children with sensory dysfunction for a long time (over 15 years) and have been challenged, not only by their sensory issues, but by time spent chasing down "appropriate" programs, services, and diagnoses. It has not always been easy, but it certainly has been a learning process for us. Instead of being tempted to simply judge and move on, we now look at our children, and other children, with a more caring and analytical eye. As teachers, our multiple credentials and certifications have allowed us to teach in public and private schools. We have taught general education classrooms, special education classrooms ("self-contained" and "inclusion"), and in integrated settings from early intervention through 12th grade. As we strive to gain new knowledge and experience, we also strive to bring our expertise and compassion into our work.

We hope you read this book with an open mind and an open heart. This book is not intended to be diagnostic, scholarly, or judgmental. This book is about possibilities and potentialities and things to ponder and to consider regarding sensory issues or sensory integration dysfunction. This book is about being authentic and realistic when dealing with children, families, and schools. We want to recognize and acknowledge that your "reality" can be very different depending on your circumstances. For example, you might be in the position of affording private schools, private therapists, and designing a "sensory room" for your child. Or you might be in the position where your child attends an under-funded school, one occupational therapist services the entire district and your three kids share a bedroom. Different issues face parents and teachers depending on whether they are in a rural, suburban or urban setting. And we realize that most people are doing the best they can under the circumstances they find themselves in. It is our experience that in most cases teachers and parents want what they feel is best for a child, whatever that may be.

Our focus in this book is to create a greater awareness of the behaviors and symptoms associated with sensory integration dysfunction and sensory issues, and to empower people by providing information. We are all about giving concrete strategies that are designed to be as effective, efficient, and practical as possible. We feel compelled to say right here, right now, that this book is *not* about looking at every behavior as a "sensory issue" or seeking services for every child with a mild "sensory issue." Rather, we will focus primarily on the children with a high enough degree of sensory dysfunction that it interferes with learning, relationships, and other skill development. Most likely, these are the kids who will need some type of strategies or interventions. These are the kids who will often receive some services, a classification, and a diagnosis of some kind. Whatever it is you are looking for, we hope this book helps you in finding it.

The ultimate goal

Our ultimate goal is for each child with sensory dysfunction to reach his or her potential.

From a parent's perspective, this may be happiness, academic achievement, friends, popularity, athleticism, membership in groups or clubs, a driver's license, college, marriage, owning a home, having a family, or a fulfilling career. Or it may be daily living skills, basic communication skills, a friend, an IEP diploma, supported employment, a good nearby group home, adaptive sport to participate in, being invited to social gatherings, or having somewhere to go for the holidays. In this book, we assert that many parents will benefit from developing a "framework" for dealing with the decisions, goals, and direction for the lifetime of their child. The parental goals for a child at 7 months old, 7 years old, 17 years old, or 27 years old and beyond will change and evolve; just as with any child. Parents plan ahead and do their best, then try to be flexible with whatever actually comes along.

From a teacher's perspective, success may mean academic success, behavioral compliance, appearing happy, acceptance by peers, positive attitude, strong work ethic, supportive family, participation in extracurricular activities, and attendance at school functions.

With the parents' and teachers' perspectives in mind, the question then becomes, how will each adult in a child's life craft the framework for a plan that is considered to be achievable, functional, and realistic, and will contribute to a child's internal compass: who she is, where she is going, and how she is going to get there. Often children with sensory processing difficulties exhibit sensory distortion, which can contribute to a strong sense of internal disorganization.

The ultimate goal of this book is to help children with sensory dysfunction and the adults in their lives gain a better understanding of themselves as they attempt to understand the world around them. We hope that this book provides useful information and insights to help in achieving this goal.

In the following chapters, we will discuss some ways to tease apart what might be attributed to sensory dysfunction, the importance of early identification, and possible home and school strategies and interventions. As you read this book, we encourage you to reflect on your own personal framework regarding sensory integration and possible dysfunction…what you already know, what you already are doing, and what information may be most helpful to you.

Chapter 1

What is Sensory Integration?

Sensory integration is a child's ability to feel, understand, and organize sensory information from his body and his environment. In essence, sensory integration sorts, orders, and eventually puts all individual sensory inputs together into a whole brain function. When the functions are whole and balanced, body movements are highly adaptive, learning is easy, and "good" behavior is a natural outcome. Sensory integration is also reflected in a child's development, learning, and feelings about himself. The connection between sensory integration and social and emotional development should not be underestimated! How a child integrates through the sensory systems provides a basis for his reality. *Not your reality, not my reality, his reality—and his unique perspective on the world around him.*

A brief history of sensory integration

About 35 years ago, A. Jean Ayres, an occupational therapist, was working with children and adults with neurologically based disabilities, when she began to realize that some of the difficulties her clients were experiencing were going beyond obvious physical impairments to subtle attention difficulties and learning difficulties that were impacting all areas of their lives—school, community, and home. Dr. Ayres began to focus her efforts on these children with perceptual learning and behavioral problems that could not be attributed to known causes. She believed that the best answers would be found in a better understanding of how the brain processes sensations—not only from the eyes and ears, but from the other parts of the body as well. Dr. Ayres believed that sensory integration occurs automatically in most people, so we just take it for granted. While many people have now become used to thinking of the brain as directing all activity in the body and mind, the concept of sensory integration continues to introduce a new way of looking at learning and behavior.

Briefly, in her book *Sensory Integration and the Child* (1979), Dr. Ayres described the nervous system as an interconnected network of nerve cells that are distributed throughout the body. The brain and the spinal cord together are known as the central nervous system. Basically, the central nervous system is responsible for taking in sensations from outside (and inside) the body, sending signals to the brain where they are organized and processed, where a response is formulated and "sent." So, according to Dr. Ayres,

> Sensory Integration is the organization of sensation for use. Our senses give us information about the physical conditions of our bodies and the environment around us. Sensations flow into the brain, like streams flowing into a lake. Countless bits of sensory information enter into our brains every moment...the brain locates, sorts and orders sensations—somewhat as a traffic policeman directs moving cars. When sensations flow in a well organized or integrated manner, the brain can use those sensations to form perceptions, behaviors and learning. When the flow of sensations is disorganized, life can be like a rush hour traffic jam. (pp.4–5)

So, it is sensory integration that attempts to "put it all together" and that helps us make sense of who we are and the world around us.

For us, as mothers, *Sensory Integration and the Child* was a challenging but incredibly eye-opening book. It gave us a lifeline—finally, someone who seemed to understand our children and give us an explanation for why they behaved the way they did. It truly changed the way we viewed our children and their "odd" behaviors. This was our first realization that our children were simply wired differently, and that there was something we could do about it. We figured that if we could just gain an understanding of sensory integration dysfunction, it would enable us to interact more positively and effectively with our children and become better advocates for their needs; and, most importantly, there was hope that we could improve the quality of their lives! We came to find out that our children were not just "willful" and "difficult," but were doing the best they could from moment to moment. Dr. Ayres was one of the first to recognize that some children's nervous systems are just not as stable as other children's, making them more emotionally fragile; that too much noise, confusion, demands, changes in routines, or illness can cause them to lose control of their emotions. It was important for the people in their lives to sense when this was going to happen and help our children to cope.

Other current theory and practice surrounding sensory integration appears to illustrate several common principles that we think are also important to note. These include:

- The central nervous system seems to contain a degree of plasticity. In other words, certain areas of the brain may be able to compensate or take over functioning for another part. For example, a toddler suffers a head injury and loses his speech; the plasticity of the brain may be able to kick in, with the toddler ending up with near age-appropriate language development.

- Sensory integration usually develops sequentially and hierarchically (the old adage…you have to crawl before you can walk, you have to walk before you can run). For example, you have to have hand and mouth awareness and a functioning pincer grasp before you can feed yourself finger foods.

- People have an "inner drive" to attempt to organize their ability to integrate and will often seek sensory input subconsciously. For example, a child may suck her thumb or twirl her hair to calm herself and regroup.

- Sensory input influences adaptive behaviors. These behaviors may, in turn, generate additional sensory-based behaviors. For example, a child is learning to swing. He learns that by "pumping" his legs harder, the swing goes higher and he begins to experience a different degree of sensory input or "swinging" movement.

Sensory processing

Sensations are the way that we take in information from our environment (internally and externally) and then process them to make sense of what is going on in us and around us. What makes sensory processing so complex is that it is not an all or nothing "thing." No one is really perfect at sensory processing, and most people have some ability to integrate through at least some of their senses. An example of someone who might be considered to possess good sensory processing might be an Olympic gymnast. An example of someone who might be considered to possess poor sensory processing might be an individual with severe autism. So, in essence, we are looking on a sensory integration "spectrum"—sensory processing along a continuum. To help people gain a better understanding of how sensory input is processed, professionals often break sensory processing down into different components; for example, *sensory registration, sensory modulation,* and *sensory response.* To clarify these terms, we will refer to sensory registration as the conscious or unconscious perception of one or more sensory signals; sensory modulation as the modification or alteration of the perception of a sensory signal (e.g., level of arousal) before it is processed for appropriate action; sensory response as the behavior that is driven by the integration of the registration and modulation of the sensory input. The following provides a brief look at a few examples of behaviors you might see in a child experiencing difficulties with sensory processing.

- *Difficulties with sensory registration:* may appear under-reactive to movement or touch, can appear lethargic, may exhibit a delayed response to sensory input. Or may appear over-reactive to movement or touch, may exhibit heightened response to sensory input.

- *Difficulties with sensory modulation:* may be upset with changes in routine, have a high level of distractibility, have a high activity level, experience difficulty with transitions, or may appear "detached", "withdrawn" or "shutdown".

- *Difficulties with sensory response or "integration":* may have problems with motor planning, may have a poor quality of motor responses (especially controlled motor responses and/or "protective" responses), may have poor body awareness, may have trouble coordinating the two sides of the body.

Some professionals include *sensory defensiveness* when addressing some of the common sensory processing problems. A child showing sensory defensiveness may resist or even strongly refuse certain types of activities or touch, may appear to be very emotionally labile or "fragile," may be considered to have "odd" or "unusual" eating habits or be considered a "picky eater" or a "difficult" child at meals.

In other theories, sensory processing has been broken down into different components. For our purposes, we prefer to break down sensory processing into the following components:

- registration of sensory input
- orientation to sensory input
- interpretation of sensory input
- organization of a response to the sensory input
- execution of response.

It is important to note that these components in sensory processing will be influenced by several other factors, including the modality (the channel it took), the intensity (how strong it was), the duration (how long it lasts), and the location (where it occurred) of the sensory input.

Understanding the role and importance of sensory processing can become increasingly important as you begin to take a closer look at behavior with perhaps a different approach to interpreting it. Two examples:

A 6th grader, Michael, is standing in line waiting for a turn at the water fountain after gym, when another student accidentally brushes his shoulder (sensory registration). Now, Michael has to figure out where on his body this sensation came from (orientation), then decide what it was—an accidental brush, light tap, hit, punch, or stab (interpretation). Michael perceives this sensory input as an accidental brush and pauses to glance behind him (organization of a response). Michael then continues to wait for his turn (execution of a response). How might you have interpreted this behavior if you had not considered the importance of sensory processing? How might you interpret this behavior now? Is it the same? Is it different?

A 6th grader, Marco, is standing in line waiting for a turn at the water fountain after gym class when another student accidentally brushes his shoulder (sensory registration). Now, Marco, has to figure out where on his body this sensation came from (orientation) and then decide what is was...accidental brush, light tap, hit, punch, or stab (interpretation). Marco perceives this sensory input as a hard punch in the middle of his back. So, Marco quickly spins around with a clenched fist in the air (organization of a response). Marco loudly and furiously threatens to find the kid who punched him and punch him back (execution of a response). How might you have interpreted this behavior if you had not considered the importance of sensory processing? How might you interpret this behavior now? Is it the same? Is it different?

WHAT IS SENSORY INTEGRATION? 19

Sensory integration is what turns sensation into perception. Perception defines reality to an individual! Again, sensory integration defines reality, *not your reality, not our reality, his reality—and his unique perspective on the world around him.*

The sensory systems

Most people are familiar with the five senses:

- touch (or tactile)
- smell (or olfactory)
- taste (or gustatory)
- hearing (or auditory)
- seeing (or visual).

However, some people remain unfamiliar with the sensory *systems*: tactile, vestibular, and propioceptive. Not only is it critical that these sensory systems function properly, but also that they work well together. If the tactile, vestibular, and proprioceptive systems cannot function efficiently, either separately or together, it directly affects a child's ability to interact successfully within him or herself, with others, and in his or her surroundings.

The tactile system

The tactile system is our sense of touch. This system allows us to feel hot/cold, sharp/dull, rough/smooth. The tactile system allows us to find (discriminate) objects by touch (feeling around in an overloaded purse for a set of keys). This information also includes light touch, pain, and texture and pressure. To better understand this, hold out your hand with your palm facing the floor and tickle the back of your hand. Now, turn your hand over and tickle the palm side. Notice a difference in your sense of touch? For most people the palm has a much higher degree of sensitivity to touch.

The vestibular system

The vestibular system coordinates the movement of the eyes, head, and body through space and body movement. The vestibular system allows us to balance, swing on a swing, coordinate the two sides of our body, and catch ourselves when we stumble. Just for fun, stand up, close your eyes, spin quickly three times in one direction, three times in the other direction, keep your eyes closed, and try to stand on one foot. That's your vestibular system at work!

The proprioceptive system

The proprioceptive system uses unconscious information from the muscles and joints to give awareness of body position. It is the feedback from muscles and joints that allow us to stand without falling, use a pencil or bounce a basketball. An example of this is to put your arm out to the side and turn your head in the opposite direction. Now bend your arm. How do you know you arm is moving? You can't see it because your head is turned the other way. You can't taste it, smell it, hear it, or touch it. You know because the sensations from your muscles and joints are giving you the information.

We believe that it is imperative to have an understanding of how sensory integration is supposed to work—how it is supposed to "look" when all the systems are up and running and working well together, in order to recognize and begin to identify the behaviors and symptoms that may indicate sensory dysfunction.

The developmental timeline

Looking back, we had early indications that our infants were struggling in the course of natural development. While we were told by family and friends that it was just a "difficult baby" or "late blooming toddler," our "gut" feelings told us that it was something more—something we didn't completely understand and something certainly we could not name. The developmental timeline provides that basis upon which many parents, caregivers, daycare providers, teachers, and pediatricians base their expectations. A look at the timeline will indicate a range of what is considered "typical" development and help begin to tease out what may be an early indication of "atypical" development.

The following is an informal timeline for birth to age 5. It is not meant to be regarded as a rigid timetable for the acquisition of skill development; rather, it is our way of providing some general guidelines to create a greater awareness of skills generally considered to be within the "normal" range of child development. This timeline is a compilation of many different developmental guidelines and our direct observations. We present the information with the understanding that cultural norms vary and may influence a child's development.

0–3 months

- Responds to voice
- Vocalizes—babbles or coos when talked to
- Smiles spontaneously
- Reaches for dangling ring
- Follows movement by turning head
- Startles at loud noises
- Wriggles and kicks with arms and legs
- Raises head when lying on tummy
- Demands to be fed
- Grasps objects placed in hand
- Enjoys bath (splashes, kicks, lifts head)
- Enjoys looking at bright things

3–6 months

- Reaches for familiar persons
- Laughs aloud
- Discriminates strangers
- Picks up a cube
- Rolls from stomach to back
- Holds head up without support
- Reaches for objects
- Turns head toward sounds
- Babbles and squeals
- Plays with rattle and teething toys
- Wriggles in anticipation—frolics when played with

6–9 months

- Imitates speech sounds
- Pulls out peg
- Uncovers toy
- Stops activity when hears "no, no"
- Waves bye-bye
- Creeps or crawls
- Responds to own name
- Stands with support
- Hits two objects together in imitation
- Takes spoon-fed baby foods
- Likes to bang, throw, and drop things
- Reaches persistently for things out of reach
- Becomes interested in exploring a variety of toys
- Sits unsupported and erect for one minute

9–12 months

- Says "Mama", "Dada"
- Looks at pictures in a book
- Holds a crayon
- Uses two words besides "Mama" and "Dada"
- Indicates wants—vocalizing, reaching
- Plays "Peek-a-boo"
- Finger-feeds self
- Cruises holding onto furniture
- May be beginning to walk with or without support
- Initiates play

- Plays "Pat-a Cake", "So Big" and ball games
- Shows tenderness toward doll or stuffed animal
- Begins to show preference for toys, begins to choose deliberately
- Begins to play games with understanding

12–18 months

- Fetches or carries familiar objects
- Uses names of familiar objects
- Points to named body parts
- Follows one-step directions
- Points to pictures in books
- Plays with other children (parallel play)
- Refers to self by name
- Asks for food when hungry
- Matches familiar objects
- Recognizes reflection in a mirror
- Initiates own play activities
- Tries putting on own shoes
- Feeds self with spoon
- Lets wants and needs be known by vocalizing, word approximations, single words, reaching, pointing, grasping
- Shows things when named
- Picks up a "finger food" with pincer grasp
- Begins to show range of emotions
- Crawls upstairs on hands on knees
- Kneels without support

18–24 months

- Stacks two to three small blocks in imitation
- Walks well
- Says about ten words (18 months)
- Listens to short stories
- Says about 25 to 50 different words (24 months)
- Concentrates intently while playing with toys
- Likes to lug, dump, push, pull, and pound
- Carries and hugs soft doll or teddy bear
- Enjoys blowing bubbles, nesting toys
- Can string a large wooden bead
- Can manage small indoor steps and slide
- Imitates adult activity
- Seats self in small chair
- Walks downstairs with one hand held
- Indicates a wet or soiled diaper

24–30 months

- Sometimes uses two-word phrases
- Copies another child's play
- Walks up and down stairs with help (two feet per step)
- Can do simple inset puzzles
- Likes pull toys, push toys, pile-up toys, sandbox, water play, hammering toys, hidden object toys
- Joins in nursery rhymes and songs
- Shows and imitates names for additional body parts
- Names common objects
- Helps put things away

- Associates use with objects
- Observes other children at play and joins in briefly
- Recognizes self in photos
- Plays simple group games like "Ring around the rosy"
- Is eager for new toys
- Begins to exhibit a capacity for "pretend" play
- Plays relatively well with older children
- Imitates more of the adult behaviors
- Is not yet able to share own toys without adult assistance
- Much play is accompanied by words
- Likes building with blocks, taking them down, filling and dumping containers, taking things apart, and putting things together
- Prefers action toys—trains, telephones, cars, riding toys
- Can fit several different shapes into shape sorting box
- Stacks five rings on spindle in correct order
- Plays happily with different textures, temperatures
- Participates more in self-dressing

30–36 months

- Can point out three items in a picture
- Can sort objects by one category (color, size, shape)
- Knows the concept of one
- Can select an appropriate object from a group of many when asked
- Begins to develop independence from parents
- Begins to develop sense of humor, plays tricks
- Begins to learn to take turns

- Toilet-trained
- Can feed self (using spoon) without help—may still be messy
- Can button and unbutton
- Engages in more "pretend" play
- Play expands—boxes, musical instruments, puzzles, blocks, etc.
- Enjoys climbing through tunnels, playing in tents (sheet over table), having a basket to carry things in
- Talks to and can be understood by unfamiliar people
- Uses three-word (or more) sentences
- Becomes conversational
- Kicks a ball
- Names body parts
- Strings large objects
- Copies simple letter formation strokes

The fourth year (ages 3–4)

- Shows preferences for certain activities (trikes, blocks, art, puzzles, sports)
- More sophisticated dramatic play
- Can take turns
- Completely dresses self (not tying shoes)
- Balances on one foot
- Names some colors
- Counts three objects
- Is curious about the "why" and "how" of things
- Emerging literacy (looking at labels, a book is more than just pictures, etc.)
- Matches and sorts by size, shape, color

- Knows stories, rhymes, and jingles, and is anxious to repeat
- Asks questions
- Is aware of feelings of self and others
- Begins to use fork effectively
- Language easily understood by unfamiliar listeners
- Conversational
- Strong food, play, and activity preferences

The fifth year (ages 4–5)

- Has definite opinions about toys, likes, and dislikes
- Enjoys dressing up like superheroes
- Enjoys scissors, jigsaw puzzles, a wider variety of toys
- Traces or prints names
- Counts from one to ten (or beyond)
- Expanding pre-literacy and pre-writing skills
- Follows through on project more than one day
- Participates in complex, sustained dramatic play
- Is becoming competitive
- Can dress and undress self without guidance
- Toilet-trained day and night
- Ties shoes
- Begins to use knife
- Follows three- or four-step directions
- Draws a person with six to eight body parts
- Conversational reciprocity, speech intelligibility near 100%
- Cooperative play

- Catches a bounced or thrown ball, can track or kick a moving ball
- Knows part or all of his address

Social and emotional development and sensory integration

Earlier in the book, we made reference to the role that sensory integration plays in social and emotional development in children. Often social and emotional behaviors provide valuable clues that a child may be experiencing sensory integration issues or dysfunction. Two areas of social-emotional development that immediately come to mind are temperament and social interaction. By reflecting on the following questions, you may gain a clearer understanding of how sensory issues may be affecting a child's social and emotional development.

Temperament

- What is the level of intensity of the child's emotional reactions?
- What is the child's level of persistence when involved in an activity?
- What is the child's activity level?
- How quickly does the child respond to changes in routine?
- What is her level of attention span/attention to task?
- How sensitive is the child to things in her environment?
- How regular is this child about self-care skills, sleeping, eating, etc.?
- When meeting new people, going to a new place, or trying something new, what is the child's reaction?
- How would you describe the child's moods? How long do they last?

Social interaction

- What is the level of affect? (Does the face express a wide range of emotions easily and freely?)

- How does the child generally respond to his parents, peers, others?

- What type of cues, if any, does the parent give to provoke a response?

- Does the child initiate interactions with parents, peers, others?

- What is the child's awareness of others?

- Does the child reciprocate in interactions with parents, peers, others?

- What types of activities does the child engage in with parents, peers, others?

- How does the child separate from parents, familiar adults, familiar places?

- Are the child's behaviors considered age-appropriate?

- Does the child have any anti-social behaviors?

- What is the child's response to a group setting, activity?

Development as viewed through a sensory lens

We would now like to begin to set the stage for looking through a sensory lens at child development, children's behaviors, communication, and learning. Again, this timeline is not rigid, rather it is reflective of the fact that each child is unique. What is considered "normal" achievement of these milestones and "typical" behavior can run the gamut. For example, a child may walk at 9 months or 15 months, a child may be very active or very quiet. These would be considered as occurring within the normal range of development. While knowledge of the developmental timeline may indicate potential developmental delays for a child, it may not necessarily "red flag" those more subtle qualitative issues. Therefore, when we look at child development, the question is not simply "Can he do this?" but "How does he approach it and perform the task?"…what is the "quality" of the performance? For example, a two-year-old is expected to be able to run well without falling down frequently. Now, how about the three-year-old that can "run" but the only way he can turn or stop is to fall down, and the only way he can run is fast? Or how about the three-year-old who is able to "run" but takes forever to cross the yard, with arms flailing, who stumbles, but never actually falls?

Basically, the developmental timeline itself, though it gives a "range" for milestones, will not necessarily reflect these "qualitative" differences in performance when assessing skill development. It is our opinion that the evaluators (parents, caregivers, daycare providers, teachers, or pediatricians) need to be keenly aware of the "quality" of the skill that they are assessing. This is critical for the child with sensory dysfunction. How about the two-year-olds in the above paragraph who both ran without falling? If the evaluator is "going by the book," then they both get that skill checked off as "achieved." However, if the evaluator (parent, teacher, etc.) is looking at quality, the picture changes considerably.

Now let's take a look at some scenarios using that sensory lens.

- A five-month-old baby is able to drink from a bottle (skill achieved). However, the bottle has three holes poked in the nipple and it took the baby over an hour to drink 4–6 ounces. Is this skill *really* achieved?

- A 28-month-old toddler is saying two- and three-word phrases (skill achieved). However, the words are less of an actual response, and more of a parroting back of the last few words the other person just used. "Jillian, would you like a drink?" Jillian responds "Like a drink." Is the skill *really* achieved?

- A three-and-a-half-year-old boy is in his preschool program and is observed to play in a variety of learning centers (skill achieved). However, the child has been wandering around the room, stopping to watch others play, never fully participating or conversing. Is this skill *really* achieved?

- A kindergartener is able to trace or print her first name independently (skill achieved). However, her grasp alternates from a mature to an immature grasp, she has a very light touch, the letters are huge, with many letters formed from the bottom up. Is the skill *really* achieved?

- A 5th grader is observed to sit quietly and attend throughout the morning's activities (skill achieved). However, the child was slouching, slumping, sliding under the desk, constantly shifting in his seat and is unable to answer content follow-up questions. Is this skill *really* achieved?

- An 8th grader is observed to get to class and get seated on time (skill achieved). However, he arrives without his homework or a working writing utensil, and he forgot his portion of the group assignment that was supposed to be worked on that day. Is this skill *really* achieved?

- An 11th grader, who is characterized as "charming, calm, and compliant" in the classroom; stressors appear to be within "normal range"—under control (skill achieved). However, in anticipation of changing classes, she becomes anxious, looking at the clock frequently, breathing rate increases—anxiety is setting in! She is waiting for the teacher to tell the class to "pack up your gear," for the bell to ring, and is straining to hear and copy down the homework assignment. How is she going to get to her locker, the bathroom, and maneuver through the noisy, crowded halls?—she actually feels sick just thinking about it. Is this skill *really* achieved?

What we are attempting to illustrate is that there are many different levels of observation and interpretations of behaviors and skills. We are saying that assessment of sensory dysfunction is the marriage of an art and a science. There is a huge difference between an evaluator/observer who is competent, and an evaluator/observer who is savvy and insightful, who is able to look beyond the superficial attributes into the complexities of the assessment process, and the uniqueness of every child. Looking back, we now see the difference between those who had the "art" down (tuned into the child, warm and fuzzy, interactive with the family, genuinely caring), or those who had the "science" down (great clinicians, superior mastery of the subject material, current in their field, able to write a detailed report), and those who *had both*. And, to be truthful, there were times when we needed "warm and fuzzy", and times when we really needed someone who would give us the cold, hard facts. And then, there were the evaluators/observers who were able to combine the art and the science to truly understand our children and their sensory issues—the challenging, and the unique as well as their individual areas of strengths and weaknesses.

Chapter 2

What is Sensory Dysfunction?

Signs and symptoms

Now, let's take a look at what occurs when a portion of the process of sensory integration is not functioning effectively and efficiently. It may show up in learning, attention, coordination, activity level, developmental difficulties, poor self-esteem, and behavior, but it *will* show up.

The following is a checklist of possible signs that a child may be experiencing difficulties with sensory integration. This is not meant to be inclusive, but rather an overview of the more common indicators of possible sensory integration dysfunction. The following information represents an expansion of our initial understanding of the signs and symptoms of sensory dysfunction that appeared in *Unlocking the Mysteries of Sensory Dysfunction* (Anderson and Emmons 1996).

- Overly sensitive to touch, movement, sights, or sounds
- Under-reactive to touch, movement, sights, or sounds
- Activity level that is unusually high or unusually low
- Difficulties with coordination
- Delays in speech or language skills
- Delays in motor skills (fine and/or gross)
- Difficulties with academic achievement
- Poor self-concept

- Difficulties with executive functioning
- Challenging behaviors

Overly sensitive to touch, movement, sights, or sounds

The child is easily overwhelmed by colors, textures, smells, sounds, or touch (particularly unexpected or light touch). This may manifest as covering eyes or ears, holding nose, gagging, vomiting, screaming, refusal to move (or could seem "frozen"), or refusal to participate in certain movement activities (loves the slide but hates the merry-go-round), or dislike of bathing, brushing (teeth, hair), and other self-care activities.

Under-reactive to touch, movement, sights, or sounds

These are the children who may crash, jump, thump, whack things (people), head butt, throw themselves, spin, rock, and generally seek means of sensory stimulation. These are the kids who, if one sensory experience is removed, will often quickly replace it with an equally intense sensory experience (e.g., four-year-old girl pedals a trike repeatedly into a brick wall, remove trike and child begins to "crash" into other kids).

Activity level that is unusually high or unusually low

This is the child who is all over the place (high level of diffused energy) or the child who is lethargic and everything appears to be a huge effort.

Difficulties with coordination

These are children who may be experiencing difficulties with fine motor activities or gross motor activities, and often both. Frequently, balance is impaired and motor planning is poor. It could be that the skills are present, but the quality of those skills is of concern.

Delays in speech or language skills

Many people are unaware of the different components of speech, such as receptive language, expressive language, pragmatics, articulation, fluency, voice, oral/motor (see p.62 for an explanation of these terms). Delays may be seen in one or more of these areas.

Delays in motor skills

Muscle tone, flexibility, quality of movement, safety with movement, fine motor, hand–eye coordination, visual perception, personal care, and upper extremity development may be delayed, diminished, or impaired.

Difficulties with academic achievement

A child's performance in one or more academic areas may, or may not, be truly reflective of his or her ability.

Poor self-concept

According to Dr. Ayres, there are three things that can contribute to a negative self-image: "the way in which the nervous system is functioning, the feelings of frustration and inadequacy that arise when a child cannot do things well and other people's negative reactions to what the child does" (1979, p.161).

Difficulties with executive functioning

This is the child who appears to lack internal organization—may be unable to keep a neat desk, locker, or bedroom, has difficulty planning ahead and having the things needed for an activity, basically disorganized and easily confused, frequently needing assistance in order to bring tasks to completion.

Challenging behaviors

Challenging behaviors often include non-compliance, "runners," "hiders," inflexibility, aggression, "shut down," low frustration level, easily over-whelmed, low tolerance for the behaviors of others, low/high activity level, physical proximity issues, perseveration (repetitive behaviors).

Dysfunction in the sensory systems

Now that you have a basic understanding of the mechanisms underlying the sensory systems, as well as the basic five senses, we are artificially dividing the sensory systems and their functions into separate categories in order to make them easier to understand. However, please keep in mind that the systems should work together simultaneously and cooperatively. In fact, if any one system does not work properly either by itself, or in conjunction with the others, it may result in a sensory dysfunction of some kind. The degree of sensory dysfunction, whether it manifests as merely a "sensory issue" or mild, moderate, or severe sensory dysfunction, is highly dependent on which senses and/or sensory systems are impaired, and to what extent. We will talk more about this a little later in this chapter, but please keep in mind as you read, that it is the integration of these systems (along with the senses) that ends up defining how we, as individuals, perceive the world around us and how this translates into how we feel and behave. We will also take a look at how dysfunction in the sensory systems may translate into social issues and behavioral difficulties and difficulty achieving age-appropriate skills development for a child. Again, the sensory systems actually operate in conjunction and cooperation with one another, so the resultant behavior or sensation is probably the outcome of accessing more than one system.

Dysfunction in the tactile system

A problem or inefficiency in the tactile system may manifest in a variety of ways. A child may be tactilely defensive and *not* want to be touched, bumped, or hugged, or to touch certain textures or wear certain types of clothes. An "atypical" tactile system may also cause a child to *crave* certain tactile sensations and experiences: never able to keep hands to themselves, constantly touching and feeling the people and/or things around them, absolutely needing to have clothes feel (or not feel) a certain way. In other words, the tactile system greatly influences relationships, fashion sense (clothing choice), and school performance.

Dysfunction in the vestibular system

A problem or inefficiency in the vestibular system may cause difficulty with balance, coordination, and motor planning. This may manifest as the child who is clumsy and uncoordinated. This may be the child who strongly dislikes gym days because she knows she is giving 110 percent, but struggles anyway—kickball, jump rope, etc. all require large amounts of motor planning and appear to be fun for most of the other kids. How frustrating! This may be the child who craves one type of vestibular input (swings), but is very afraid of slides or bikes; or the child who is embarrassed because he cannot even figure out how to get on a skateboard and ride for 30 seconds, let alone learn the great tricks his friends are learning to do on their skateboards. This may also be the child who is willing to ride the bus for hours (loves it!), or the child who has a meltdown every morning at the bus stop. In other words, the vestibular system will play a key role in the ability of a child to participate successfully at sports, in gym class, on the playground, and in various activities at school and at home.

Dysfunction in the proprioceptive system

This refers to an inefficiency in the proprioceptive system that may cause a child to have difficulties both at school and at home. Since the proprioceptive system gives feedback from the muscles and joints, it supports holding a pen or pencil correctly, staying properly seated in a chair, applying the right amount of pressure during a hug, or learning to use a knife, fork, and spoon correctly. This system also supports learning to walk, opening and closing jars and doors, using playground equipment and chewing!

Logan's day

Now we would like to help make all of this "academic" information come "alive." One of the most challenging aspects of sensory integration dysfunction is learning how to identify and tease apart the components of the underlying dysfunction. While each child is unique and sensory problems vary greatly in both type and degree, this section will give you a clearer idea and better understanding of the day in the life of one child with sensory dysfunction. The following is an example of some of the experiences, challenges, and interactions of a 3rd grade boy named Logan, who has sensory dysfunction.

5:45am   Logan wakes up, is chilly because he took off pajama shirt in middle of night because tag bothered him (*tactile*). Gets out of bed and heads to bathroom. Bumps into doorframe on the way out the bedroom door (*vestibular/proprioceptive*). Uses toilet, refuses to flush—noise bothers him (*auditory defensiveness*). Has difficulty turning on faucet (*proprioceptive*), can tolerate only cold water (*tactile*) and forgets to use towel to dry hands—don't "feel" wet. Heads downstairs to eat and watch video.

6:00am   Stumbles on steps, but does not fall (*proprioceptive/vestibular*). Goes into kitchen and pulls out pre-prepared breakfast (Mom and Dad want to sleep until 6:30!). Logan will only eat a peanut butter and strawberry jam sandwich and a glass of Welch's grape juice for breakfast (*gustatory*), he refuses cereal because he cannot stand "crunchy" food (*texture/auditory*).

6:15am   Eight-year-old sister comes downstairs, tells Logan to wipe the jam and grape juice off of his face and chest—Logan did not realize he had spilled food on himself (*tactile/proprioceptive*). Logan bumps into sister when getting towel (*vestibular/visual*). Yells at sister for being in his way.

6:20am   Mom comes downstairs and asks Logan to get dressed and to brush his teeth. Logan protests, but stomps upstairs (*proprioceptive*). Logan cannot find his shirt—which is on the top of his dresser next to his baseball glove (*visual*). Logan gets himself dressed (*proprioceptive/visual/vestibular/tactile*).

6:40am   Heads to bathroom to brush teeth. Squeezes too much toothpaste (*visual/proprioceptive*). Brushes teeth, gagging on taste of toothpaste (*gustatory*).

6:42am   Logan heads back downstairs to watch favorite video. Logan clumsily shoves the video into the VCR (*proprioceptive/tactile*) and sits mesmerized by the video he has seen at least 100 times. The sound is too loud and Mom tells Logan to turn it down a couple of notches (*auditory*).

7:30am   Mom tells Logan to turn off the video, it is time to get ready for school. After one more warning, Logan turns off the video, grabs his knapsack and goes out to wait in the car.

7:35am   Mom hands Logan his jacket and demands that Logan put it on—it is 38 degrees outside! Logan protests, saying that he is *not* cold and refuses to wear that jacket because he can't stand the sound of nylon when it "shooshes"—it creeps him out (*tactile/temperature/auditory*). Mom runs in and retrieves Logan's fleece jacket, because they are going to be late and she knows that Logan will probably not be able to find his jacket hanging in the closet with all of the other coats and jackets—even if it is right in front of him (*visual*).

7:55am   Logan and his sister are dropped off at school. Logan walks while covering his ears because he knows that the first bell will ring at 7:58am (*auditory*). Logan jostles through the throng of children, heading up the stairs to his classroom. He arrives angry because he is positive that several other children intentionally bumped him as he ascended the stairs (*tactile, proprioceptive*).

8:05am   Logan takes off his jacket and hangs up his knapsack, then sits at his desk, knocking over Sarah's chair on his way through the room. Sarah sighs in exasperation, but Logan doesn't seem to notice the sigh or the fact that he knocked over her chair (*visual/tactile/auditory*).

8:15am   Mrs. Miller asks Logan to take attendance and lunch count down to the office. Logan accidentally walks into the classroom next to the office (*visual*). Stumbles once on the steps on the way back up to his classroom—stupid steps! (*proprioceptive/vestibular*)

8:20am   Mrs. Miller asks the class to take out their math books and homework. Logan fumbles through his desk, finding everything but a pencil—it's in there somewhere, but feeling around for it inside the desk is hard! (*discriminatory touch*).

8:30am   Mrs. Miller hands out a small package of M&Ms to each student, instructing the class to open the package carefully (the class will be learning about fractions today!). Logan (and one other boy) somehow rips open his package with too much force and M&Ms spill all over, under, and around his desk (*proprioceptive*).

9:00am   Mrs. Miller instructs the class to line up for gym. Logan arrives at gym a little agitated because Robert kept "bumping into me on purpose" (*proprioceptive/visual*)—Robert and the rest of the class agree that it was Logan who stopped suddenly and was not watching where he was going.

9:05am   Mr. Rodes quickly prepares his class for a game of soccer. Once the game begins, Logan alternately stands with his hands over his ears or yells at the top of his lungs (*auditory*). There is too much movement (*visual*) and noise (*auditory*), Logan is overwhelmed (*sensory overload*) and begins to meltdown, crying and yelling.

9:40am   Mrs. Miller tells the class to get into their assigned groups and work on their social studies project. Logan becomes agitated as the noise level of the room rises (*auditory*), he speaks loudly and almost knocks over the diorama! (*visual*).

11:45am   The children go to the cafeteria for lunch. Logan sits with his classmates at their assigned table. Throughout lunch, Logan "slides" off the bench (*proprioceptive*), stuffing his lunch into his mouth (*proprioceptive/tactile*). Logan always has the same lunch (*texture/gustatory*), and gags if he smells tuna fish (*olfactory*).

12:15pm The children go from the cafeteria to the playground for recess. Logan runs to the swing and spends the entire recess swinging—as he does every day (*vestibular*).

12:45pm The children go back to the classroom and sit quietly while Mrs. Miller reads a book aloud. Logan rocks gently in his seat while listening intently (*vestibular/proprioceptive*).

1:05pm Mrs. Miller instructs the class to line up for art. Logan complains loudly that he hates art—the room smells awful (*olfactory*), and he hates touching the weird paper, paints, and brushes (*tactile*).

2:40pm The whole school gets ready for dismissal. Logan hurries past the buses because they are too loud (*auditory*) and smell just awful (*olfactory*), looking for his babysitter's car. Janet, the sitter, tries to park in approximately the same place every day, because she knows that Logan has a hard time finding her car amid a line of cars (*visual*). If he can't find her, he will panic.

3:05pm Logan eats his usual snack of raisins, a cheese stick, and a Welch's grape juice box. He usually has difficulty opening the cheese stick and unwrapping the straw for the juice box (*proprioceptive*). Logan and his sister and playmates go outside to play. Logan usually swings by himself, he hates the slide and isn't very good at catch (*vestibular/visual*). The other kids don't like to play tag with Logan because he pushes too hard when he tags them (*tactile/proprioceptive*).

4:45pm Dad arrives to take Logan and his sister home. Logan requests a bear hug (*proprioceptive/tactile*).

5:00pm Logan works on homework while Dad starts dinner. Mom walks in the door just as Logan starts to rip his homework paper. Logan tearfully screams, "I can never get the stupid numbers to line up, so my answer is always wrong!" (*visual*).

5:30pm Dad calls everyone to the dinner table. Logan runs to the table, stubbing his toes on his chair (*vestibular*). Logan grumbles as Mom hands him his plate of macaroni and cheese, peas, carrots, and apple sauce. Logan won't eat the apple sauce—it's too chunky (*texture*) and Mom forgot to scrape the breadcrumbs off of his macaroni and cheese (way too crunchy) (*texture*).

6:00pm   Logan leaves the kitchen covering his ears because the noise of the dishes clattering bothers him immensely (*auditory*).

6:30pm   Logan goes to karate class. Logan loves being in his bare feet on the hard floor (*texture/proprioceptive*) and being able to chi up (yell) loudly (*auditory*). This form of karate, *suh bahk do,* is non-contact so he doesn't have to worry about touching people too hard (like in games of tag).

7:45pm   Mom tells Logan to get ready for his shower. Logan gets the water just the way he likes it—Mom says it's so cold, she thinks Logan is part penguin (*tactile/temperature*). Sometimes Logan forgets to rinse his hair or to towel off after showering—he just doesn't feel the shampoo on his head, or the water dripping from his body (*proprioceptive/texture*).

8:00pm   Mom and Dad tuck Logan into bed, but Logan won't be able to sleep because his bed has the scratchy sheets. Mom and Dad realize that Logan will be up and unable to sleep, so they quickly change his sheets to the soft, comfortable ones he likes (*texture*).

8:15pm   Mom and Dad hear Logan rhythmically rocking back and forth in his bed (*vestibular/proprioceptive*).

9:25pm   Logan falls asleep.

11:30pm   Logan awakens and needs help falling back to sleep.

Keep in mind that no child (or adult) has perfectly integrated sensory systems all of the time. Sensory issues will vary within any child throughout the day, depending on specific environmental circumstances and physiological state. Certainly, feeling tired, hungry, or sick will greatly affect how our sensory systems work and how our brain interprets the incoming information from our sensory systems. Growth spurts and hormones also affect the way a child's body responds to sensory input. However, a child who has sensory integration dysfunction will have relatively specific and predictable sensory issues, while it may not appear so initially. Notice that Logan was very sensitive to loud noises (*auditory sensitivity*) that he could not control, but if he was the one in control of the noise, "loud" was fine. Also, certain textures were an issue throughout the day, as were specific temperatures and taste aversions/preferences. It is also important to note here that certain activities involving specific sensory systems were either craved in an obsessive manner (*swinging—vestibular*) or avoided at all costs.

Sensory dysfunction through the developmental stages

Now, let's explore the different stages of life, newborn through school age and beyond, and how sensory integration dysfunction may present. For the purposes of this book, we are describing a wide range of behaviors and symptoms that may indicate some level of sensory dysfunction. These lists are not meant to be used for diagnostic purposes, rather to create a greater awareness of some of the sensory difficulties a child may experience over the course of development.

Newborn to age one year

Typically, most bets are off when it comes to diagnosing a child at this early stage. However, in a retrospective kind of a way, first-year behaviors and developmental milestones become quite germane when assessing the developmental history of a child for sensory dysfunction. Please keep in mind that *most* babies will present with one or more of these characteristics for a (relatively) short period of time. The basic difference is that a "typical" baby will gradually become more self-regulatory—eating, sleeping, playing, and crying within reasonable (and tolerable) limits—colicky babies eventually stop being so intensely fussy and irritable, the sensitive baby who "startled" at every little noise stops being so "jumpy" as her/his nervous system matures. An infant who has sensory dysfunction probably did not pass through the more difficult "phases" with a gradual ease. In fact, chances are quite good that such an infant was a difficult or "different" baby, who somehow remained "intense" and "difficult" throughout the first year of life.

POSSIBLE SENSORY SIGNS AND SYMPTOMS

- Chronic crying
- Almost never cries
- Inability to develop a reasonable sleep pattern
  - sleeps too much
  - only sleeps for very short periods of time (power naps)
- Dislikes being swaddled
- Only likes a certain texture or material close to skin
- Overwhelmed by relatively low amounts of noise

- Appears to be oblivious to noise, even loud noises

- Nothing seems to "startle" him

- Everything seems to "startle" him

- Dislikes being touched or held

- Demands to be held or touched constantly

- Bare feet not able to tolerate the texture of carpet, bare floor, etc.

- Gross motor milestones are late or have not yet occurred, e.g., rolling from tummy to back and from back to tummy, sitting up unsupported, grabbing for rattle or toy, creeping, "army crawling" or crawling

- Fine motor milestones are late or have not occurred yet, e.g., sucking independently, holding bottle or cup, tracking faces and objects, grasping objects with hands, attempting to pull off socks, hat, bib

- Continued, intense reaction (vomiting, screaming) to certain textures or tastes of food or drink

- Craves certain smells

- Very aversive to certain smells

- Craves certain sensory input: swinging, sliding, jumping, thumping

- Very aversive to certain sensory input: swinging, sliding, jumping, thumping

ADDITIONAL POSSIBLE SIGNS AND SYMPTOMS AS SEEN IN THE COMMUNICATION, SOCIAL, AND EMOTIONAL DOMAINS

- Is not particularly interested in faces

- Is not particularly interested in social games (peek-a-boo, smiling, silly faces)

- Poor or intermittent eye contact

- Does not babble

- Unable to be comforted (rocking, singing, walking, swinging)

- Much more interested in objects (or parts of objects) than in people

- Acts as if "deaf"

- Constantly jabbers

- Will only "play" with one or two specific toys—always in the same manner (e.g., only interested in clapping blocks together or pressing the button on a toy or watching things spin)

OKAY, WHAT MIGHT IT LOOK LIKE?

Does the infant need to be held, walked, or rocked all day? Or does the infant scream when being picked up, rocked, or riding in the car? Does he calm when touched, stroked, or massaged? Or does she scream when being held, having a diaper changed, or being dressed? Does the infant respond to bright colors, bright lights? Or is he under-responsive or looks away from them? Does the infant seem unbothered by sudden loud noises? Or does she scream, become frantic, or become rigid when the doorbell rings, someone knocks on the door, the telephone rings, or you turn on an appliance? Some infants, for example, will nurse or drink a bottle without event; while others may have a sucking reflex described by one mother as like "a Hoover vacuum on high" or may take hours to nurse or drink from the bottle. Some infants take 20-minute "power" naps throughout the day (never connecting two hours of sleep). Or they sleep anywhere, anytime for extended periods of time on a fairly regular schedule.

Most parents and pediatricians agree that many of the behaviors seen in babies tend to be ephemeral and only become "diagnostic" when viewed through the lens of time. There are exceptions to this, of course. For example when a baby has a physical problem such as prematurity, an infection, a hernia, deafness, or blindness, which makes him fussy, irritable, or unable to process sensory stimuli. Pediatricians are trained to rule out such physical illnesses and ailments in infants. In most cases, however, after the appropriate medical screening, parents are told to relax, and that their baby is simply going through a difficult phase, or is a very sensitive baby.

The toddler

Most toddlers are tumultuous and terrific, changing gears seamlessly and frequently. Toddlerhood is a time of explosive physical, cognitive, social, and emotional growth. The child who was a helpless infant only 18 months ago, is now attempting to climb up onto the kitchen counter and explore the sink! The world is calling to the toddler, and the toddler is eager to respond.

Again, in retrospect, the signs of sensory integration dysfunction are often evident during toddlerhood. However, the "typical" toddler has many transient behaviors, which will most likely wax and wane, but will eventually regulate themselves over time. Again, the "typical" toddler will transition into a preschooler, who is much more mature (comparatively) and who has an improved ability to self-regulate. The toddler who has sensory integration dysfunction will most likely present with behaviors that remain quite toddler-like as she ages into a preschooler. The "play" of a toddler who has sensory integration dysfunction is usually qualitatively very different from his typical counterpart. This is also the time when the characteristically uneven skills of the child who has sensory integration dysfunction often become much more noticeable.

POSSIBLE SENSORY SIGNS AND SYMPTOMS

- Tantrums frequently and intensely (constant sensory overload)

- Craves certain sensory stimulation (sounds, textures, smells, feelings)

- Aversive to certain sensory stimulation (sounds, textures, smells, feelings)

- Inability to develop a reasonable sleep pattern
    - may have very irregular or disjointed sleeping patterns
    - may wake up at same time each morning regardless of the time she goes to bed the night before

- Loves/hates certain sounds (toilet flushing, coins dropping, vacuum cleaner, etc.)

- Very sensitive to sounds or crowds

- Aversive to being touched or held

- Constantly has hands all over everything or everyone

- Craves certain sensory input: swinging, sliding, jumping, thumping

- Aversive to certain sensory input: swinging, sliding, jumping, thumping
- Continued, intense reactions (screaming, vomiting) to certain textures or tastes of specific foods or drink
- Appears so engrossed in activity of the moment that she seems unaware of the people or activity around her
- Delays/difficulties in gross motor skills
- Not playing with toys that require fine motor manipulation
- Not feeding self easily or well
  - no orientation to spoon or cup

ADDITIONAL POSSIBLE SIGNS AND SYMPTOMS AS SEEN IN THE COMMUNICATION, SOCIAL, AND EMOTIONAL DOMAINS

- More interested in adults than other children
- Limited interest in faces
- Limited social game playing (peek-a-boo, smiling, silly game faces)
- Unusually distractible
- Intense powers of concentration for certain activities
- May not point, or only points infrequently
- Talks incessantly/rarely
- Poor or intermittent eye contact
- More uncomfortable in new situations for a longer period of time than would be expected
- Insists on routine, or tantrums and melts down
- Flat affect (face does not express a wide range of emotions easily or freely—poker face)
- Monotone or sing-song voice

- Will only play with a very few selected toys—always in the same manner (spinning wheels on cars, pressing buttons, "dumping" blocks, listening to vacuum cleaner or other motors)

- Intensely interested in one subject to the exclusion of virtually all other subjects (construction equipment, a specific cartoon character, specific book, or specific species of animal)

Most parents will only recognize these "symptoms" in hindsight and seek help for their child when the child becomes older and the characteristics are persistent or intensified. Frequently, however, parents will feel uneasy about their child's development and perhaps seek professional advice, only to be told to "wait it out." Often parents are told that "things" (i.e., behaviors) will improve as the child grows and becomes more emotionally mature and more socialized. The advice typically given to the parent is to have the child join a playgroup and to keep introducing new experiences gradually, but consistently.

The preschooler

The typical preschool child is fun-loving, inquisitive, and social. Preschoolers are raring to experience new sights, sounds, and situations (as long as a trusted adult is in sight). Preschoolers are able to walk, talk, argue, and think independently, they begin to play cooperatively with their peers, and make their opinions known to all! Most three- and four-year-olds love to laugh and learn new things and have begun to understand many complex social rules and many of the "rules of language" (pragmatics of language). It is at this age that many parents of a child with sensory processing difficulties become even more confused, because those "odd qualities" in their child that were supposed to fade are often still present, or even amplified.

POSSIBLE SENSORY SIGNS AND SYMPTOMS

- Unusually anxious

- High tolerance of pain

- Low tolerance of pain

- Still has not developed a reasonable sleep pattern (too much or too little)

- May wake up at same time every morning, regardless of bedtime the previous night
- Tags/clothing/textures bother him
- Very picky eater
    - certain textures/tastes/temperatures of food are aversive or craved
    - does not know when he is "full"
    - vomits or gags easily (does not tolerate certain foods well)
- Very sensitive to noise around him
- May act oblivious to noise or confusion surrounding him
- Craves or has aversions to certain physical activities
    - proprioceptive: jumping, stairs, hopping, lifting heavy things
    - vestibular: swinging, spinning, rocking, sliding
    - tactile: hates to be touched, or has hands all over everyone and everything, insists on certain textures
- Persistent drooling
- Strong preferences for or aversions to specific playground equipment
- "Chewer"—shirts, blankets, toys
- Clumsy with fine motor activities: eating, drinking, using writing utensils
- Clumsy with balance and coordination: difficulty riding and using age-appropriate toys (big wheel, trike, pull toys, tracking balls, kicking balls)
- Lack of hand dominance
- Difficulty crossing midline (the imaginary vertical line that divides the body in two): for example, using the right hand to reach an object on the left of the midline
- Hypotonic (poor posture)
- Difficulty with bilateral coordination
- Falls out of chairs

- Prefers adults to children
- Prefers to play with much younger children, or by self
- Voice modulation issues (consistently too loud or too quiet)
- Monotone or sing-song voice
- Strange rhythm to speech
- Asks constant questions, but may not wait and listen to response
- Poor or intermittent eye contact
- Emotionally labile (laughing one minute, crying the next)
- Perseverative (repeating behaviors)
- Socially "aloof" with peers/socially intense
- Rarely or never points
- Easily overwhelmed
- Strange quality to "play" with other children
- Inflexible; insistent on routine—may become frantic if routine is altered
- May only play with a very few selected toys—always in the same manner (spinning wheels on cars, pressing buttons, "dumping" blocks, listening to vacuum cleaner or other motors)
- Limited interest in playing with toys outside of his area of interest
- Intensely interested in one subject area to the exclusion of virtually all other subjects (construction equipment, a specific cartoon character, specific book or specific species of animal)

As the preschooler ages, strange proclivities and odd behaviors may begin to really stand out. Often, because the child with sensory integration dysfunction has unevenness of skill development, parents, grandparents, caregivers, preschool teachers, and pediatricians may be apt to downplay the child's weaknesses and focus primarily on the child's strengths.

The school-aged child

Now is when, as the saying goes, the rubber meets the road. The child with sensory integration dysfunction may remain on that border of being considered a bit odd, but still within the realm of "normal," or, most likely, will cross over into the realm of displaying some (a few, many) problematic behaviors. Often the child with sensory integration dysfunction will be categorized as immature and, possibly, "spoiled".

The new social, cognitive, and motor demands of the school setting often create even more confusion, anxiety, and chaos for the child who has sensory integration dysfunction. Remember, all the sensory systems need to be working well cooperatively for higher skills acquisition and performance! All too often, the only way the child has of dealing with this environment is to "space out," act out, and become *more rigid, inflexible, anxious, and socially challenged!*

POSSIBLE SENSORY SIGNS AND SYMPTOMS

- Over/under-sensitive to pain
- Over/under-sensitive to temperature
- Shouts or whispers most of the time
- Becomes wild or confused and "lost" during recess
- Certain noises bother her to an extreme degree
- May have difficulty keeping hands to herself
- Constantly touching other students or objects
- May complain frequently of being bumped and touched by other students
- Unable to focus—eyes and attention are "all over the place"
- Slides out of seat easily, attempts to lie down or sprawl, frequently "slumped" over desk—looks like a "rag doll" at times
- Is aversive to sight, smell, or taste of certain foods
- Acts "grossed out" or may gag when touches certain textures (paint, glue, sand)
- Unable to tolerate certain types of clothing or tags, or the sounds certain clothing makes (e.g., nylon rubbing on nylon)
- Is clumsy—tendency to bump, trip, bang into things
- Difficulty prioritizing sensory stimuli

- Executive functioning issues emerge or become amplified
- Social skills deficits may become more obvious
- Behavioral immaturity
- Impulsivity
- Unusually picky eater
- Difficulty during lunch—managing time, opening container independently, messy eaters, meticulous eaters
- Need for higher level of adult supervision for a variety of reasons (management, social, academic, organizational)
- The lethargic student
- Hyperactivity
- Identification of learning disabilities
- Visual-motor difficulties
- Distorted sense of weight (a light bag of groceries may feel very heavy)
- Diminished strength and endurance
- Over-dressing or under-dressing for the weather
- Pronounced trouble with changes in routines or plans
- Difficulty making choices when confronted with several options
- Falls apart easily over seemingly minor occurrences
- Articulation problems
- Oral/motor issues (needs to chew all the time, drools, or hates to brush teeth, may loathe going to the dentist)

Often, at this point, the child with significant sensory issues may become more frustrated with himself and more challenging to those around her.

The functional areas as viewed through a sensory lens

Now that we have looked at the developmental timeline and its sub-categories (cognitive, language and communication, motor (including vision and hearing), social/emotional, and adaptive), we have established that sensory integration is a component embedded within all domains. We suggest that in assessing each sub-category, it is critical to identify the sensory components within skill development.

Delay or disability in cognitive development

The child demonstrates deficits in intellectual abilities beyond normal variations for age and cultural background. These difficulties might be in ability to acquire information, problem solving, reasoning, generalizing of information, rate of learning, processing difficulties, memory delays, and attention or organizational skills.

What might this look like in the child with sensory integration dysfunction? In our view, it is very difficult to tease apart the sensory component in cognitive development. For our purposes here, we are going to consider cognitive development (not strictly IQ) as a combination of the acquisition and mastery of communication, memory, and adaptive skills development.

Delay or disability in language and communication

The child demonstrates deficits beyond normal variation for age and cultural background that adversely affect the ability to learn and acquire skills in the primary language. These difficulties might be in receptive language, expressive language, articulation/phonology, pragmatics, fluency, oral/motor skills or voice (sound quality, breath support).

What might this look like in the child with sensory integration dysfunction? A baby with sensory issues in the area of language and communication may:

- take a long time to respond (or doesn't respond) even to a familiar voice

- need his name called several times before responding

- scream at unexpected noises, crowded places, or just when alone (screaming is his only way to tell you something is not "right" in his world)

- give poor or little eye contact

- not be interested in faces

- not attempt to imitate sounds (babbling).

A toddler with sensory issues in the area of language and communication may:

- have a very flat affect (not beginning to show a wide range of expressions: happy, sad, surprised, puzzled)
- sometimes act as deaf, even though hearing tests out as normal
- continue to chew and eat non-edibles
- stuff her mouth with food, gag, choke on a regular basis
- continue to drool copiously
- rely on screaming, gesturing, vocalizing to communicate needs/wants
- have difficulty following simple directions
- have difficulty pointing to or naming common objects when asked
- tantrum frequently and intensely.

The preschooler with sensory issues in the area of language and communication may:

- have difficulty responding appropriately to what is heard
- have difficulty following one-step directions (group setting) and two-step directions (individually)
- have difficulty responding to the comments and questions from others
- have difficulty answering simple questions/asking simple questions
- be difficult to understand when speaking
- have tantrums that are frequent and/or intense.

Delay or disability in adaptive development

The child demonstrates difficulty in learning or acquiring the skills necessary for daily living and learning through play. These occur over time, in a variety of situations, and interfere with the effectiveness of the child's ability to meet personal needs, social responsibility, or participation in developmentally appropriate situations and cultural group.

What might this look like in the child with sensory integration dysfunction? A baby/toddler or preschooler with sensory issues in the area of adaptive development may:

- not like being cuddled
- over-react/under-react to changes in temperature and textures
- over-react or under-react if hands, face, clothing and/or diapers (excessively soiled underpants in older children) are messy
- have difficulty sensing, or overly sense the urge to urinate or defecate
- become agitated when being bathed (hair washed, face wiped)
- have poor body awareness and/or poor motor planning as seen in difficulties with self-dressing, feeding, and other adaptive behaviors
- not be developing age-appropriate play skills
- have difficulty in many functional areas out in the community (shopping, visiting relatives/friends, playgroups, children's museums, libraries, etc.)
- be under/over-reactive to pain.

Beyond the age of five, children typically become much better at compensating for their sensory issues because they have such a strong desire to "fit in" with their peers, so the adult must look even more closely at the behaviors of the child who may:

- continue to be over-reactive/under-reactive to changes in textures and temperatures
- continue to avoid self-care activities (bathing, combing hair, washing face, clipping nails, dressing, teeth brushing, flossing, shaving, feminine care issues)
- have difficulty sensing, or overly sense the urge to urinate or defecate
- continue to be under/over-reactive to pain
- continue to have poor body awareness and motor planning.

Delay or disability in social/emotional development

The child demonstrates deviations in affect or relational skills beyond normal variation for age and cultural background. Problems are exhibited over time, in various circumstances, and adversely affect the child's development of age-appropriate skills.

It is our opinion that the evaluator from each discipline should consider making note of and including the social/emotional elements during assessment. This could be included in the narrative portion of the evaluation, and may provide some of the most valuable information regarding the child's level of sensory processing and sensory dysfunction.

What might this look like in the child with sensory integration dysfunction? Typically, this will be seen as problems with:

- greeting others
- play with peers
- role in a dyad
- ability to handle conflict
- attention span
- choices/self-mastery
- adaptability
- reactivity
- affect
- responses to request
- awareness of self/others
- reciprocity
- social participation.

Delay or disability in motor development

The child demonstrates a deficit beyond normal variability for age and experience in coordination, movement patterns, quality or range of motion, or strength and endurance of gross (large muscle), fine (small muscle) or perceptual motor (integration of sensory and motor) abilities that adversely affects the child's ability to learn and acquire skills. These skills may include maintaining and controlling posture, functional mobility (walking, running), sensory awareness of the body or movement, overall sensory integration, reach and grasp of objects, tool use, perceptual motor abilities (eye–hand coordination for tracing), and sequencing motor components to achieve a functional goal.

Assessment and evaluation

Becoming a "sensory" detective

People often ask, "What constitutes sensory integration dysfunction or a sensory processing disorder? When do we know the child has sensory integration dysfunction? What is the difference between a sensory issue and sensory dysfunction?" These are good questions and this remains a somewhat complicated issue. First of all, sensory integration dysfunction by itself is not a clinical diagnosis, according to the DSM-IV (American Psychiatric Association 2000). Which, translated, means that there are no blood tests or biological markers, so basically it requires a health professional (usually an occupational therapist or a physical therapist) working from an observational checklist marking off specific indicators under specific categories. Second, the term "sensory integration dysfunction" is often used interchangeably with "sensory dysfunction" and "sensory processing disorder," making things confusing at times. And frequently sensory integration dysfunction is concurrent with diagnoses such as autism spectrum disorder, cerebral palsy, Down syndrome, ADHD, learning disabilities, etc. However, it has been our experience as teachers (special education and general education) that sensory integration dysfunction is most often a co-condition with another diagnosis. Only rarely have we encountered a child with a straight diagnosis of only sensory integration dysfunction.

Again, it is our belief that there is significant difference between sensory integration dysfunction and a mild sensory issue. For us the bottom line is: "Are the sensory difficulties impacting daily living, relationships, learning, and behavior; and, if so, to what degree?" Here is where we need to talk about degree and quality. Now, for a four-year-old who is exhibiting "typical" behavior in every other area but refuses to put her hands in the sandbox, is this really a big problem? Is it really pervasive? Is it really adversely impacting her life? Could it be that this is just a "stage" or something ephemeral? In other words, will she grow out of this? And, does it really matter if she does? (There are plenty of adults who do not like to get their hands dirty.) However, if she doesn't like to put her hands in the sandbox, *and* gags when she touches glue or finger paint, *and* falls out her chair, *and* the slide terrifies her, *and* her mother has intense daily power struggles with her about what she is going to wear and what she is going to eat, *and* is obviously overwhelmed by large group activities, *now* do we have a big problem? Is it pervasive? Is it impacting her life/learning/social development? Maybe. At this point, as parents and as teachers, we would want to take a closer look at this child's level of previous experience and exposure to these types of activities. If lack of exposure and experience can be ruled out as a strong contributing factor, then we would recommend to this child's parent that she receive further evaluation while at the same time begin to kick into gear some sensory-based strategies to help this child's individual needs.

Gathering and documenting information

If, as a parent or a teacher, you suspect that a child (or your child) has significant sensory issues or sensory integration dysfunction, you now become the detective. Now is the time to start documenting your dealings with the inevitably complicated array of service providers, and gathering information that will be useful for a professional assessment.

Okay, now that you have got your detective hat on, what you are going to need is some time and a focus. Next up is a notebook; decide what will go into that notebook, and start thinking who you might share it with. As parents, we found it useful to write down the dates, phone numbers, and a brief, general description of whom we spoke to and about what.

Here's an excerpt from Polly's first notebook:

3/28/94

Called Carol (Initial Service Coordinator from Early Intervention Agency). Not in today, left message, will call back tomorrow.

Called Sue (speech therapist) regarding evaluation comments on Dylan's echolalia. States that it is found predominantly in autistic children. Asked if I would agree to a "Psychological." I asked directly if he would receive speech services. Sue advises "no," but he would be evaluated at regular intervals.

3/29/94

Carol calls back. States she will contact Mary (Committee on Pre-school Education Chair) regarding Dylan's speech services and aging out of preschool special education services. Carol said she will contact Robin (Physical Therapist Evaluator) and see if she has enough concerns to recommend that Dylan receive physical therapy services. Carol calls back in the afternoon saying that she spoke with Mary (CPSE Chair) and that Dylan will not receive any summer services or services next year unless he is enrolled in Kindergarten.

Called Barbara to verify this information (is this true?). Barbara states that if Dylan is recommended and approved for a 12-month program, CPSE must provide services through August.

This example is *really* from Polly's first notebook. She was a concerned mom who was struggling to understand what was going on, and the rules and the regulations, and just wasn't always getting consistent information. This may not be what an excerpt from your notebook will look like, but it gives you an idea of how important it is to document times, dates, people and information so that it can be referred back to—even years later. Can you believe that this speech therapist would throw out that a child she just evaluated may have autism, recommends a psychological evaluation, and does not initially recommend speech services? Honestly, as it turned out, some of Dylan's and Ellie's best allies have been some incredibly committed and compassionate therapists and Sue, this speech therapist, was eventually one of them.

In addition to documenting communications and conversations, you will want to start documenting behaviors. It is imperative to note the specifics of the behavior: What does it look like? How long did it last? How often does it happen? And where does it happen? For instance, mentally you may have kept track that every time you walk into a grocery store with your child he has a super-sized "meltdown." So, now you want to actually look at the behaviors and write down what the "meltdown" looks like... Johnny is smiling and happy entering the store, but once he gets near the carts he starts pulling his hand away from yours and starts screaming. You have learned that you cannot physically force him into the front seat of the cart, but if you hoist him into the back of the cart he spends about a minute and a half thumping his feet against the bottom of the cart and then stops screaming—gravitational insecurity (anxiety caused by, for example, feet leaving the ground, movement and heights)? We don't know, but it is worth keeping track of. Now that you think about it, he melts down getting him into his car seat too (which looks like arching his back, screaming "no, no, no" and pushing you away with all of his might). Is there a connection? We don't know, but it's worth keeping track of.

And now after the grocery shopping, Johnny is being dropped off at pre-school and you are his teacher. Initially, you may assume that Johnny is "being difficult" because his mother usually looks stressed out and you figure that they had a tough morning. Mentally, you have kept track that Johnny has difficulty sitting, attending and on the playground. But when you begin to write the behaviors down, you are surprised to see a pattern developing. Johnny never has difficulty at circle time (sitting on the floor), but he screams and thumps his feet when he sits at the chairs at the art table (the taller chairs) intermittently until the activity is over. And while Johnny loves to run around on the playground, he refuses to go anywhere near a swing—gravitational insecurity? We don't know but it is worth keeping track of.

Now when Johnny's parents and teacher have a parent–teacher conference, both parties can now share specific and well-documented concerns with observations and examples. Writing down observations serves valuable purposes for both parents and teachers...and most importantly for the child.

The communication log for the parent then may reflect:

4/6/04

Met with Johnny's teacher, Ms.Taylor, for a parent conference. We shared our concerns about Johnny's behavior at the grocery store (screams, refuses to sit in front of cart, thumps feet in back of cart) and in the car (screaming, non-compliance) and that these behaviors seem to occur when he is forced to take his feet off the ground. Ms. Taylor shared that Johnny's behavior at school is more challenging (screams and thumps feet) when he sits in the taller chairs and that he also refuses to go on the swing.

Here are just a few ideas to get you started taking a closer look at possible sensory-based behaviors. Let's begin by having you answer the following questions...

- How does this child respond to
    - being touched by others, touching others?
    - different types of clothing?
    - different textures?

- activities that involve self-care (brushing teeth, washing, bathing, hair combing, nail clipping, shaving, feminine care)?
- different types of foods (temperature, taste, texture, presentation)?
- having his feet off the ground?
- having his head upside down during play or sports?
- different types of movement activities?
- his surrounding environment (people, things, noises, smells, visual stimulation, etc.)?

- What is your child's attention span?
- Physically—does he tire easily, or never slow down?
- What is his choice of physical activities? Activities that involve grasping and/or manipulating objects?
- How does he respond to being around other people?
- How does he respond to changes in routine?

Childhood development experts seem to agree that the earlier the identification and intervention for sensory integration dysfunction is begun, the better. If we know that the first few years of life are the most important time for brain development for a "typically" developing child, then we know that these years are critical for a child with "atypical" development. Some disabilities will be detected either immediately or shortly after birth, other will take a few weeks. However, while sensory integration dysfunction is apparent early on, it often goes undetected for months or years. It is not uncommon for a child with sensory integration dysfunction to reach preschool age or even school age before being identified. How can this be?

Unfortunately the identification of children with sensory integration dysfunction most often depends on the knowledge and experience of the adults in their lives. There will be children who have a diagnosis where the sensory piece is either underestimated or overlooked. Other children who may be exhibiting the behaviors and symptoms commonly associated with sensory integration dysfunction may get the "wait and see" approach or be missed altogether. Some of these children may meet the criteria of another diagnosis, possibly an autism spectrum disorder; others may not (see Chapter 3).

The role of assessment

The role of the assessment process is critical to beginning to target the needs of the child. We believe that early and accurate identification of any need is essential in order to give the child the potential for best possible outcome. And it is our belief and experience that many times it is the sensory component (to whatever degree) that is overlooked or undervalued. That having been said, we want to recognize that the assessment process can have many drawbacks—cultural bias, artificial setting, purposeless tasks—and is sometimes used for purposes for which it was not intended. In addition, we also want to recognize that there can be the over-representation and under-representation of certain racial and ethnic groups in special education. However, this is the system that is currently used and we must work within it as we work to improve upon it.

In general, whether done formally or informally, the purpose of assessment is to take a closer look at a child's development in five areas: cognitive (learning) skills, language and communication skills, motor skills (including vision and hearing), social/emotional skills, and adaptive skills. There are many different ways to assess children, just as there is a wide variety of assessment tools available. Assessment can be formal, using standardized testing, or informal, making use of observation using checklists, rating scales, etc. Assessment may be done informally simply to note progress over time in an area of skill development. Or assessment may be done formally to determine if the skill levels are deficient enough in any one area, or combination of areas, to warrant further investigation.

The assessment process can be broken down into logical steps. What we want to do is to highlight the tremendous importance of each step in the process.

- Identifying a possible need will determine which, if any, evaluations should be performed (pediatrician referral, parents, etc.).

- Evaluations, if any, will assess the need and determine whether any additional evaluations are warranted. For example, the parents make a referral because they have concerns about their child's speech. The speech therapist evaluates the child. Now is the time for the speech therapist, or any other initial evaluator, to look beyond his or her specific discipline at the *whole child* to determine if any other needs, sensory or otherwise, exist and to make the recommendation for any supplemental evaluation. Often, this is a matter of professional awareness and judgment.

- The assessment(s)/evaluation(s) will help determine which, if any, interventions are needed.

- The level of intervention needed will help determine which services, if any, should be provided.

- The services, if any, will help determine a child's program.

- A program will help determine how the child's needs will be met through, for example, related services, curricular adaptations, environmental modifications, management needs, teacher training, etc.

It all starts with the identification of a child's need and the assessment of this need. It is our belief that the "sensory piece," if any, needs to be identified and assessed as early as possible to ensure that it is incorporated into any intervention, service, or program.

Traditionally, sensory integration has been the exclusive realm of the occupational therapist. Now we see signs that this is starting to change and although it is still the occupational therapist who will do much of the formal, standardized testing for sensory dysfunction, other disciplines are beginning to recognize sensory integration dysfunction, make referrals for further evaluations, and incorporate a "sensory approach."

ASSESSMENT TERMINOLOGY

We feel that "knowledge is power" and that by gaining a better understanding of assessment terminology and the different types of assessment, you can become a better advocate for your child and a more active participant in the assessment process.

Psychological evaluation: Looks at whether an individualized program/special education is needed, determines IQ (Intelligence Quotient), looks at behavior and makes recommendations regarding behavior management. In older children it looks at academic achievement.

Social history: Looks at the background information for illnesses, surgeries, medications, birth history, developmental milestones, family history, and previous school experience.

Audiology: Looks at the child's ability to hear, middle ear function—determines the absence/presence of middle ear fluid (which can affect speech) and refers any possible ear infections to a physician.

Speech/language evaluation: Looks at

- receptive language—understanding what is said
- expressive language—use of language to express ideas
- pragmatics—"rules" of social language/communication
- articulation—how clear a child's words are
- fluency—smoothness of speech, rate of flow
- voice—quality and pitch of sounds (hoarse)
- oral/motor—structure of the mouth.

Physical therapy evaluation: Looks at

- muscle tone—how the muscles feel (are they tight or floppy?)
- muscle strength, posture
- flexibility—of joints and muscles
- balance and coordination
- motor skills—ball skills, jumping, sitting, climbing, running, walking, stationary movement, object manipulation
- quality of movement—whether movement is easy or difficult, variety of movement
- breathing patterns
- safety with movement.

Occupational therapy evaluation: Looks at

- upper extremity development—using arms/hands in a coordinated manner
- fine motor skills—performance of activities that require more refined hand/finger movement and hand–eye coordination skills
- visual-motor skills—the ability to use motor skills to copy designs that are presented in a picture
- personal care skills—hygiene, toileting, self-dressing abilities, self-feeding (how the structures in and around the mouth are working)

- visual perception—how a child perceives the visual world around her through her non-motor responses (looking not moving), looks at visual memory, visual discrimination, visual figure-ground and visual closure
- sensory functioning—how a child reacts to the information that she is receiving through her senses and sensory systems
- vision—provides an informal visual screening to identify possible concerns that may require further evaluation by a specialist.

Criterion-referenced tests: These tests compare a student's performance with a previously established criterion rather than with other students from a normative sample. "Normative" means, for example, in comparison to other children the same age.

Norm-referenced tests: These tests use normative data for scoring which include performance based on age, gender or ethnic group.

Individual assessments: This type of assessment is usually a discipline-specific evaluation performed by one member of a multidisciplinary team (speech therapist, occupational therapist, physical therapist, psychologist, special education teacher, etc.) using both formal and informal assessment strategies.

Arena style evaluation: A multidisciplinary team composed of professionals from various disciplines (occupational therapy, physical therapy, speech therapy, child development, psychology, etc.) evaluates a child. Team members usually develop an evaluation plan prior to the actual evaluation so the same behavior can be observed from several perspectives simultaneously. With this technique, usually one member of the team facilitates interaction with the child while the other team members observe and document the child's performance across a variety of assessment domains. The child's presenting needs will drive the composition of the assessment team.

Formal assessment: Standardized assessments are specific tests that measure specific skills, abilities, and domains. Results are reported in a statistical manner—percentiles, age equivalents, grade equivalents, criterion-referenced, norm-referenced, etc.

Informal assessment: These are non-standardized assessments such as checklists, rating scales, interviews, observation, or performance-based assessment. They often draw upon "professional judgment" using observations presented in a narrative, as anecdotal or supporting information.

Programs and services

Early intervention (Newborn to age three years)

Our focus as we look at the role of the evaluator, and the evaluation process, will be on early intervention and preschool-age programs and services. That is not to take away from the importance of school-age evaluations, programs and services, but to emphasize the key role of early identification and early intervention concerning sensory dysfunction. Honestly, we feel strongly that this is where things need to start being "put together" and happening. Unfortunately, by the time a child enters mid to late elementary school the emphasis shifts strongly to accommodation and behavior management.

In general, early intervention agencies/programs are designed to support children to age three and their families in a variety of areas, including health and wellness and child development, with one of the goals being for children to acquire age-appropriate skills and be "ready to learn." The goals of the early intervention programs are driven by family concerns and family goals. In your area, there may be opportunities for young children to receive a developmental screening through, for example, primary care providers, newborn intensive care units, follow-up programs, etc. One role of early intervention programs is to offer supplemental screenings or further evaluation opportunities for children with a suspected developmental delay or disability. So, if you have a child whom you suspect may have sensory integration dysfunction or significant sensory issues, we encourage you to discuss this with your pediatrician, local early intervention program provider, or your school district. We also encourage parents to be present and participate in their child's developmental screening whenever possible. There is no doubt in our minds that parents have proven, and continue to prove, that they are the single most accurate source of information regarding their child and that they should always be welcomed as partners in the provision of all early intervention services.

EARLY INTERVENTION EVALUATIONS

In many areas, children suspected of having a developmental delay may be referred to an early intervention agency/program, and may be entitled to a multidisciplinary evaluation.

A multidisciplinary team (sometimes referred to as multifactored) is generally made up of qualified individuals who have sufficient expertise and the credentials to assess the child's present level of performance in each of five developmental domains (cognitive "learning" development, language and communication development, motor development (including vision and hearing), language and social/emotional development, and adaptive skills development).

Preschool-age services (Children ages three to five years)
DEVELOPMENTAL SCREENINGS

General education developmental screenings become significantly more utilized during the preschool years. For example, a preschool program may decide to provide developmental screenings to every child in their program. Here the purpose may not just be to identify children with possible developmental delays, but to identify those children "at risk," or to note progress over time in a "typically" developing preschooler. Here, for example, a screening tool may be administered by a general education preschool teacher at the beginning and end of the school year to note progress for parent/teacher conferences. As more and more early intervention programs come under increasing pressure to provide outcome-based documentation of student progress to help justify funding for the program, we also see an increased use of screening tools. One benefit of the developmental screening is that it is usually easy to administer (some training required), does not take long to administer, and can provide valuable information as to how a child is developing in one or more domains. The developmental screening can also help provide to families some more concrete documentation (rather than just opinion) for a teacher or child development specialist who feels a recommendation for further evaluation is warranted.

SOME BASIC COMPONENTS OF THE INDIVIDUAL EVALUATION

The purpose of this evaluation is to determine the child's present level of performance and if the child is eligible for any programs or services. The evaluation of a preschool child requires both information gathering from parents, etc., and the administering of individual evaluations. These evaluations should include a formal assessment, behavioral observations, and parent/caregiver and/or teacher interview.

Ideally, individual evaluations should be written in a timely manner in parent-friendly terminology, in the family's primary language. The evaluation could include:

- behavioral/clinical observations

- relevant background information

- significant temperament and personality traits (in the context of the child's behavior)

- test scores

- description of needs/strengths

- evaluation findings.

SOME THOUGHTS ON ELIGIBILITY

Since there is that wide range of variation in early child development and skill acquisition among children, this needs to be taken into account when considering the potential eligibility of a preschool child for a special education program and/or services. We feel that it is important for the parents, caregivers, and teachers of a child with a suspected developmental delay or disability to understand what the functional areas are and what skill deficits may be considered when eligibility is considered. Ultimately, eligibility may be determined relative to months of delay, percent of delay, and standard deviations, or a diagnosed medical condition. In a nutshell, whether you are a parent of a child with sensory integration difficulties or the teacher of one (or, as in our case, both), we feel it is imperative that you gain an understanding of how your educational system works, what functional areas are of concern, whether the assessment tool used was appropriate to determine the present level of performance, and whether, ultimately, it gave an accurate picture of the child's needs.

Significant sensory issues or sensory integration dysfunction are not necessarily going to be represented on many standardized assessment tools outside of the occupational therapy/sensory domain. Therefore, parents and professionals may need to search within the assessed areas for patterns, behaviors, and deficits that may indicate sensory dysfunction and eligibility for services.

Chapter 3

Concomitant Diagnoses

Sensory integration dysfunction is often referred to as a "hidden disorder." As moms, and now, as teachers, we get quite a laugh over that nickname—the "hidden disorder." However, you may find that once you are familiar with the behaviors and symptoms of sensory integration dysfunction, it is usually about as "hidden" as an ostrich with its head in the sand or the grape juice stain all over the front of the brand new, dazzling white t-shirt! These kids virtually scream "sensory dysfunction" in a variety of settings (school, home, Grandma's, the grocery store, McDonald's, etc.) in their lives. In fact, when one really stops to think about it, that is what makes it sensory dysfunction—it appears to be the way their sensory systems work. Unfortunately, sensory dysfunction does not take a vacation, nor does it "stay quiet" and not manifest just because it is Grandma's birthday and the whole extended family is at a fancy restaurant.

It is our understanding that sensory integration dysfunction is rarely clinically diagnosed as a "stand alone" disorder, but is typically described and diagnosed as concomitant (coexisting) with another diagnosis, or as an interwoven feature of another diagnosis. We feel it is important to gain an understanding of some of the more common diagnoses that sensory integration dysfunction or sensory issues may be associated with, or embedded within.

The following is a listing of the more common diagnoses and/or conditions that may have sensory issues or full-blown sensory integration dysfunction associated with them.

- Autism spectrum disorders
- ADD (attention deficit disorder); ADHD (attention deficit hyperactivity disorder)
- Down syndrome
- Cerebral palsy
- Traumatic brain injury
- Fragile X syndrome
- Mental retardation
- Premature birth
- Substance abuse by mother during pregnancy
- Fetal alcohol syndrome
- Angelman's syndrome
- Bipolar disorder
- Oppositional defiant disorder
- "Emotionally disturbed"
- Conduct disorder
- Obsessive-compulsive disorder (OCD)
- Learning disabilities
- Reactive attachment disorder

Again, this illustrates that sensory integration dysfunction is typically part of a "larger picture," and just because a child has received another diagnosis, does not necessarily rule out sensory dysfunction. And, conversely, if for some reason the child has received a "stand alone" diagnosis of sensory integration dysfunction, it does not necessarily rule out a concomitant diagnosis.

At this point we would like to take brief look at Asperger's syndrome, autism spectrum disorders, learning disabilities, ADHD, and bipolar disorder. These diagnoses are becoming more prevalent in general education class-rooms throughout the United States, and are those where we clearly see a strong connection with sensory issues.

What is an autism spectrum disorder?

At this point we would like to address autism spectrum disorders (ASD), which exist on a continuum. We believe that in virtually all diagnosed cases of autism, there is a significant component of sensory dysfunction. The continuum ranges from PPD-NOS (pervasive developmental disorder, not otherwise specified) on the mildest end of the spectrum to severely autistic on the other end of the spectrum. However, beyond recognizing ASD as a "clinical continuum," it is personal for both of us. We want people to understand and relate to our children, and all of the children who are on "the autism spectrum." One of the primary reasons for including these DSM-IV definitions is to highlight the criteria needed for the clinical diagnosis of an autism spectrum disorder to help in early identification and early intervention, and in the development of appropriate services and individualized programming for these children. If your child appears to be exhibiting some of the behaviors consistent with these diagnoses, we recommend further evaluation by a qualified professional.

According to the DSM-IV (American Psychiatric Association 2000), pervasive developmental disorders are categorized into five types:

- autistic disorder
- pervasive developmental disorder, not otherwise specified (PDD-NOS)
- Asperger's disorder
- Rett's disorder
- childhood disintegrative disorder.

We are most concerned here with the first three of these, which are the autism spectrum disorders. The DSM-IV criteria for these three diagnoses are here set out in full (American Psychiatric Association 2000).

Autistic disorder

A. A total of six (or more) items from (1), (2), and (3), with at least two from (1), and one each from (2) and (3):

    (1) qualitative impairment in social interaction, as manifested by at least two of the following:

       (a) marked impairment in the use of multiple nonverbal behaviors, such as eye-to-eye gaze, facial expression, body postures, and gestures to regulate social interaction

       (b) failure to develop peer relationships appropriate to developmental level

       (c) a lack of spontaneous seeking to share enjoyment, interests, or achievements with other people (e.g., by a lack of showing, bringing, or pointing out objects of interest)

       (d) lack of social or emotional reciprocity

(2) qualitative impairments in communication, as manifested by at least one of the following:

       (a) delay in, or total lack of, the development of spoken language (not accompanied by an attempt to compensate through alternative modes of communication such as gesture or mime)

       (b) in individuals with adequate speech, marked impairment in the ability to initiate or sustain a conversation with others

       (c) stereotyped and repetitive use of language or idiosyncratic language

       (d) lack of varied, spontaneous make-believe play or social imitative play appropriate to developmental level

(3) restricted, repetitive, and stereotyped patterns of behavior, interests, and activities as manifested by at least one of the following:

       (a) encompassing preoccupation with one or more stereotyped and restricted patterns of interest that is abnormal either in intensity or focus

       (b) apparently inflexible adherence to specific, nonfunctional routines or rituals

       (c) stereotyped and repetitive motor mannerisms (e.g., hand or finger flapping or twisting or complex whole-body movements)

       (d) persistent precoccupation with parts of objects

B. Delays or abnormal functioning in at least one of the following areas, with onset prior to age 3 years: (1) social interaction, (2) language as used in social communication, or (3) symbolic or imaginative play.

C. The disturbance is not better accounted for by Rett's disorder or childhood disintegrative disorder.

Pervasive developmental disorder, not otherwise specified

This category should be used when there is a severe and pervasive impairment in the development of reciprocal social interaction or verbal and nonverbal communication skills, or when stereotyped behavior, interests, and activities are present, but the criteria are not met for a specific pervasive developmental disorder, schizophrenia, schizotypal personality disorder, or avoidant personality disorder. For example, this category includes "atypical autism"—presentations that do not meet the criteria for autistic disorder because of late age of onset, atypical symptomatology, or subthreshold symptomatology, or all of these.

Asperger's disorder

A. Qualitative impairment in social interaction, as manifested by at least two of the following:

   (1) marked impairment in the use of multiple nonverbal behaviors such as eye-to-eye gaze, facial expression, body postures, and gestures to regulate social interaction

   (2) failure to develop peer relationships appropriate to developmental level

   (3) a lack of spontaneous seeking to share enjoyment, interests, or achievements with other people (e.g. by a lack of showing, bringing, or pointing to objects of interest to other people)

   (4) lack of social or emotional reciprocity

B. Restricted repetitive and stereotyped patterns of behavior, interests, and activities, as manifested by at least one of the following:

   (1) encompassing preoccupation with one or more stereotyped or restricted patterns of interest that is abnormal either in intensity or focus

   (2) apparently inflexible adherence to specific, nonfunctional routines or rituals

   (3) stereotyped and repetitive motor mannerisms (e.g. hand or finger flapping or twisting, or complex whole-body movements)

   (4) persistent preoccupation with parts of objects

C. The disturbance causes clinically significant impairments in social, occupational, or other important areas of functioning

D. There is no clinically significant general delay in language (e.g., single words used by age 2 years, communicative phrases used by 3 years)

E. There is no clinically significant delay in cognitive development or in the development of age-appropriate self-help skills, adaptive behavior (other than social interaction), and curiosity about the environment in childhood

F. Criteria are not met for another specific Pervasive Developmental Disorder or Schizophrenia

See Chapter 6, "More About Asperger's Syndrome", for examples and explanations of these diagnostic criteria.

What are learning disabilities?

According to the Learning Disabilities Association of America (2005), "the term 'learning disabilities' is really an 'umbrella' term describing a number of other, more specific, learning disabilities." Some of these specific disorders include:

- dyslexia—a language and reading disability
- dyscalculia—problems with arithmetic and math concepts
- dysgraphia—a writing disorder resulting in illegibility
- dyspraxia—problems with motor coordination
- central auditory processing disorder—difficulty processing and remembering language-related tasks
- visual perceptual/visual motor deficit—reverses letters; cannot copy accurately, loses place, struggles with cutting
- nonverbal learning disorders—trouble with nonverbal cues, e.g., body language
- language disorders (aphasia/dysphasia)—trouble understanding spoken language, poor reading comprehension.

(Learning Disabilities Association of America 2005)

It has been our experience that children with learning disabilities often have an underlying sensory processing component, and that, for these children, the sensory piece should be addressed in conjunction with any prescribed strategies and treatments.

What is ADHD?

Attention deficit hyperactivity disorder (ADHD) is a condition that often becomes apparent in preschoolers and early elementary school age. For these children it is hard to pay attention and control their behavior. The principal characteristics of ADHD are inattention, hyperactivity, and impulsivity. Because many children exhibit these symptoms to some degree it is important that the child receive a thorough examination by a well-qualified professional before this diagnosis is made. According to the most recent edition of the DSM-IV (American Psychiatric Association 2000) there are three patterns of behavior that indicate ADHD. These are predominantly hyperactive-impulsive type (that does not show significant inattention), the predominantly inattentive type (that does not show significant hyperactive-impulsive behavior)—sometimes called ADD (although this is now an outdated term), and the combined type (that displays both inattention and hyperactive-impulsive behavior).

Some signs of hyperactivity-impulsivity are:

- feeling restless, often fidgeting with hands or feet, or squirming while seated

- running, climbing, or leaving seat where quiet behavior is expected

- having difficulty taking turns or waiting in line

- blurting out answers before hearing the whole question.

Some signs of inattention are:

- often becomes easily distracted by irrelevant sights and sounds

- has difficulty following directions, loses personal items, forgets things needed for certain specific tasks

- has difficulty paying attention to details, makes careless mistakes

- often moves from one uncompleted task or activity to another.

It has been our experience that many children with a diagnosis of ADHD have an underlying sensory component that may be impacting their "attention" activity level and learning. We think it is important to assess and evaluate the possibility of a sensory component in conjunction with the prescribed treatment for the ADHD.

What is bipolar disorder?

Bipolar disorder is often characterized by alternating periods of emotional highs and emotional lows. This disorder can range from mild to severe. For many people symptoms include, during a period of emotional "highs":

- feelings of euphoria, optimism
- rapid speech, racing thoughts, agitation, increased physical activity
- poor judgment
- recklessness
- difficulty sleeping
- tendency to be easily distracted
- inability to concentrate
- extreme irritability

During a period of emotional "lows", symptoms include:

- persistent feelings of sadness, anxiety, guilt, or hopelessness
- disturbances in sleep and appetite
- fatigue and loss of interest in daily activities
- difficulty concentrating
- recurring thoughts of suicide.

It has been our experience that for some children with a diagnosis of bipolar disorder there is an underlying sensory component. During periods of an emotional "high" an individual may experience a heightened sensory awareness or sensory feedback. In contrast, during a period of an emotional "low" an individual may experience diminished sensory awareness or sensory feedback.

To medicate or not to medicate...this is the question

For many families, whether to medicate or not to medicate a child is a huge issue/concern or dilemma. We feel it is a very individual, personal choice as to whether or not to medicate your child. We have seen children where medication has been useful and effective, where medication has been neither useful nor effective, and where medication has appeared to have some benefit. And we have seen families who have felt strongly opposed to medication and have opted not to pursue this as a treatment option. Our role (as parents or teachers) is not to judge; we've walked in many of those shoes, and it is not easy. This is why we feel so strongly that each parent, teacher, therapist, and physician needs to be very informed. These are big, possibly life-altering decisions that must be weighed carefully and monitored closely.

Chapter 4

Sensory Dysfunction at School

Everyone has a job to do

It is our belief that everyone working with a child plays an important role in creating an effective and cooperative partnership on behalf of the child.

The teacher's role

We encourage teachers to learn as much as possible about the child's delay or disability, and consider possible "links" to sensory integration. In doing so, teachers may want to take a new look at assessment, and begin to explore the use of adaptations and modifications for their students. In support of home and school partnerships, we feel it is crucial that teachers model an embracing attitude toward families and students. We believe all children need to witness, to feel, and to understand the benefits of tolerance and acceptance.

The parents' role

We encourage the parents of a child with delays or a disability to become advocates for your child. We would like to point out to parents that it has been our experience that most teachers are doing the best they can (often with limited training, experience, and resources). One reality may be that even the most gifted teacher can have difficulty successfully integrating a child with special needs into the classroom. Or it could be one of those instances where the teacher and the student are simply not a good "match."

What special education is, and is not

Because sensory integration is a common thread found in learning and development, children with sensory dysfunction may need the assistance of a special education teacher to accommodate these differences in learning and development. The paradigm for special education services in many countries is shifting. The following is our frame of reference regarding the role of special education services.

Special education *is:*

- a service
- providing the supports and services necessary for the student to succeed/participate
- ongoing training for all school personnel
- specific training when a classified student is included
- a diverse classroom where the fundamental components are:
  - effective teaming with other teachers, specialists, support personnel, administration, and parents
  - working knowledge of the child's educational needs
  - diverse instructional strategies
  - diverse management strategies
- reflected in an attitude of tolerance and acceptance
- each child achieving his or her potential as a student.

Special education is *not:*

- a place
- placing several classified children with a teacher (because she or he is willing to take them)—this classroom then becomes a kind of hybrid, modified special education classroom
- placing classified children into classrooms without the proper services, supports and background information
- requiring a teacher to provide a completely modified (and different) curriculum—the child who colors in a worksheet while seated in the back of the room with his or her aide, while the rest of the class works on academics
- designed to eradicate a disability.

Navigating the labyrinth of special education services can be a formidable task. However, the personal and professional satisfaction that results from understanding the system is well worth the effort. We believe that an understanding of and a respect for all students are the driving forces behind a caring and committed teacher. *Never underestimate your power to touch the life of a child!*

The "players" on a child's team

As mothers of children with sensory integration dysfunction (and concomitant diagnoses), and as special education teachers, we bring with us the parents' perspective as well as the teachers' perspective. And, not so surprisingly, we find there is much common ground. We see both parents and teachers as addressing very similar issues: directing attention, social interaction, academics, living skills, social/emotional development, task completion, and challenging behaviors.

Again it is important to realize that every school is different, and each classroom in a school is unique. Your local area may have a slightly different terminology for a specific position—in our schools, we have special education teachers. In other schools, they may be referred to as consultant teachers, or by any one of a number of titles. Thus, each child and teacher is really working within a unique environment.

Here is a listing of possible school personnel and their typical roles.

- *Teachers* are responsible for the academic curriculum, grades, classroom management, scheduling, social and physical needs of the students in the classroom.

- *Special education teachers* are teachers who have a specific certification to teach students with disabilities. The special education teacher may provide services either directly to students (classroom teacher—many are special education certified, resource room teacher, direct consultant teacher) and/or to classroom teachers and support personnel (indirect consultant teacher, resource room teacher).

- *Paraprofessionals* may be a "classroom para," who, under the supervision of the classroom teacher, assists the teacher by helping students and performing tasks in the room (e.g., gathering items for a project, daily lunch count, handing out supplies and papers).

- *1:1 paraprofessionals* are assigned to assist a specific student, and accompany that student throughout the school day. A 1:1 para will have very specific duties (as assigned by the teacher) that are designed to support the student in all situations throughout the day.

- *Speech therapists* teach language, communication, oral/motor, and social skills to students who have deficits in these areas. Therapy may be delivered inside the classroom, during an activity—this is generally referred to as "push-in therapy"—or the therapist may take the student to his or her speech room—this is generally referred to as "pull-out therapy" (because the student is "pulled out" of his or her classroom). The speech therapist is responsible for addressing the pragmatic speech deficits in a student who has autism.

- *Occupational therapists* are responsible for helping students who have recognized deficits in the areas of fine motor function, eye–hand coordination, and sensory dysfunction. OTs help students who have difficulty using their hands for school-related activities (printing, writing, using scissors, manipulating small objects) or life skills activities (buttoning, zipping, tying shoes, using eating utensils). Some OTs also help students who have been diagnosed with sensory dysfunction. Therapy may be delivered on a "push-in" or "pull-out" basis.

- *Physical therapists* are responsible for providing therapy for students who have recognized deficits in gross motor function. PTs help students who have mobility, muscle strength, and coordination issues. PTs may also treat students who have sensory dysfunction. Therapy may be delivered on a "push-in" or "pull-out" basis.

- *Adapted physical education instructors* are responsible for designing and implementing a physical education program for students who, due to their disabilities, are not able to participate in the school's general education physical education program.

- *School social workers* are usually certified (CSW—certified social worker) and/or have a Masters degree in social work (MSW—Masters in Social Work). Social workers help students work through personal, family, and social problems.

- *School psychologists* usually have an advanced degree in some form of psychology, typically child psychology.

- *School nurse.*

Analyzing possible sensory dysfunction and offering solutions

Before we analyze specific situations, let's take a look at some "basic level" problems and possible solutions. This will be helpful when it comes time to tease apart complex situations.

We will consider some of the more common areas of sensory difficulties, followed by a list of functional, practical suggestions.

Auditory dysfunction

- *Verbal warnings* help a great deal—"Class, the cafeteria is going to be noisy…"

- Student may wear *noise-muffling headphones* (now there are some very unobtrusive headphones—much less geeky).

- Allow student to listen, with headphones, to *music* that they enjoy.

- Allow student to cover ears.

- Offer a less noisy *alternative*, if possible (either a less noisy spot in the same place, e.g. the corner of the cafeteria, or sometimes a different place is available; sometimes a student can go somewhere a few minutes early, to avoid being in the middle of the din).

- Consider allowing the use of a *tape recorder* for the student to listen to a lecture or instructions again at a later time (*not* in place of listening when information is being delivered).

Tactile dysfunction

- Help student *recognize and verbalize* issues and sensitivities as much as is possible (the more the student is a part of the process, the better the outcome will be).

- If student is *tactilely defensive* (does NOT like to be touched or to touch)

- allow the child to *wear gloves*, so his skin does not have direct contact with the aversive texture
- *introduce aversive textures slowly*, allowing students to build up tolerance at their own pace (if everyone else is having pretzels for snack, but Breon finds crunchy to be aversive, ask him to try one bite (or maybe just "Hold the pretzel for a moment, then you can have your banana")
- recognize that a student may need a *cotton towel* or piece of cloth on his chair or "place on the rug" because the texture of the chair or rug is too aversive/distracting.

- Allow the student to be either the *line leader* or the line *"caboose"* (but never in the middle of the line—believe us, the complaints of being touched will begin before the class has exited the room!).

- *Gain tolerance* to textures by small, *frequent exposures* to a variety of textures (hands/feet in dry macaroni, beans, birdseed, packing peanuts, water, playdough, frosting, shaving cream, cotton, Velcro, synthetics, tacky glue, finger paints).

- If the students *crave tactile input* and have their hands all over everything and everyone
  - tell *social stories* about appropriate times and ways of touching people
  - use a *hula hoop* for establishing personal space boundaries (place hula hoop on ground, have student stand in the middle to help visualize personal space boundaries for self and others)
  - allow a *squeeze toy* or "fidget toy" (tennis balls work great!) to squeeze throughout the day
  - allow younger students to have a *small square of carpeting* or towel to *define "their space"* when seated or standing
  - have a *"hand pouch"* (two handkerchiefs sewn together) ready for student to stick hands in.

Gustatory (taste) dysfunction

- For aversions, introduce slowly, perhaps with a *sniff* at first, then slowly progressing to a *quick lick* (then spit out if necessary), then to a *bite* that is swallowed.

- For sensory cravings, sometimes the amount, place, and times need to be well defined and explained ahead of time ("Rita, you may have one cookie after breakfast, then one after you get home from school—at 3:15—these are the only two times you will get a cookie").

Olfactory (smell) dysfunction

- Attempt to have adults *not use perfume* or colognes or body lotions.

- If possible, use shampoos, conditioners, and deodorants that are not strongly scented.

- If possible, match the scents of shampoo and deodorant, so your body is not emitting a potpourri of scents.

- Try to use *art supplies and classroom supplies that are unscented* or as lightly scented as possible (unscented markers, playdough, glue, Kleenex, air fresheners).

- If a student cannot tolerate a smell that is wafting through the building (from the cafeteria, from general cleaning or painting, from the art room, etc.), attempt to remove the student as much as possible from the smell:
  - close classroom door
  - position child near open window
  - use a small fan near the child to blow the scent away (this worked the best in our classrooms and *all* of the kids loved it)
  - place a scent the child likes near the child to offset the unwelcome scent as much as possible.

Visual dysfunction

- Assess the learning environment for *placement and quantity of visual stimulus.* Every classroom needs to be a celebration of the achievements and efforts of the students—but is the classroom too busy visually? Is every inch of space taken up, creating a visual montage? Or are work, art, and projects displayed in a thoughtful manner, provoking a creative, organized atmosphere?

- Use *icons*, words, or words and icons together (mounted on index cards) to help refocus, to promote staying on task and to minimize behavioral issues.

- Use *sign language* to "back up" words and/or icons. Very useful during transitions times, classroom group time, and during large (noisy) crowd times—cafeteria, assembly, recess, physical education.

- Use *exaggerated facial expressions* (typically a child with ASD and often a child with sensory issues will not "get" the subtle nuances of facial expressions or someone who is "talking with her eyes"). Of course, the student needs to be practiced in what these facial expressions mean ahead of time—"Oh, I get it, Mrs. Emmons, that is your 'I don't understand' look!"

- Define the layout of the room by physical boundaries.

- Use real objects to define abstract ideas—e.g., *hula hoop* for space, *clock* that shows by color how much time is left for an activity (or waiting time), a *circle* that is red on one side and green on the other side (either attached to a popsicle stick or hung around the neck with yarn) that can be wordlessly flipped by the teacher or paraprofessional to indicate when a child needs to be quiet (and not interrupt), or can ask questions or volunteer information. Use realistic *manipulatives* (something that looks and feels like the actual object, e.g. small plastic coins) whenever possible.

- Consider providing the student with:
  ○ a *study guide* for a topic or lecture
  ○ an *outline* where the student is responsible for filling in the details (this works well, helping to keep the student on track and not just attempting to write down every word).

Children who have autism spectrum disorders are, overwhelmingly, visual learners. However, visual schedules will prove to be a lifeline for many students.

- *Individual schedules*—icons only, words only, icons with words, color-coded; subtly included in student's notebook, posted on board, taped to desk (inside plastic protector), carried by student, teacher or paraprofessional.

- *Classroom schedules*—icons only, words only, icons with words, color-coded, laminated, posted on board, above door, etc.

Figure 4.1 Examples of preschool-age icons for more effective transitions. Teachers may also choose to use generic photos, personalized photos or hand-drawn sketches as visual supports.

Figure 4.2 Examples of school-age icons for more effective communication

• 8:45–9:15	Science centre (rocks and minerals)
• 9:15–9:45	Reading group (Chapter 2)
• 9:45–10:00	Restroom break
• 10:00–10:30	Physical education (soccer)
• 10:30–11:00	Math group (homework p.217)
• 11:00–11:30	Work on social studies project (individual)
• 11:30–12:00	Lunch in cafeteria (pizza or cheese sandwich)
• 12:00–12:30	Playground (outside if no rain; room 15 if rain)
• 12:30–1:00	Language arts (have colored pencils out)
• 1:00–1:30	Global studies (whole class)
• 1:30–1:45	Restroom break
• 2:15–2:45	Speech with Mrs. Jamison
• 2:45–3:00	Ready for home (bookbag, homework folder)

Figure 4.3 Andrew's schedule—an example of a visual schedule using words only

Proprioceptive dysfunction

- Allowing the student to wear a weighted vest may help (easy to make), or a knapsack with some weight.

- Use a non-slip mat to prevent student from sliding out of chair so easily.

- Use a non-slip mat to hold pieces of paper or worksheets in place.

- Allow student to stand at desk at various times.

- Allow student to walk up and down stairs.

- Supply a chubby pencil grip for holding on to pencil.

- Allow student to wear an adjustable belt or waistband around waist.

- Give student a tennis ball to squeeze.

- Joint compressions may be helpful (a technique that needs to be learned from a certified OT or PT and closely supervised).

- Let student listen while sitting on a large physio-ball or T-stool.

- Let student give self a bear hug.

- Have student carry something with weight or hold a couple of books (if seated).

- A mummy-style sleeping bag to wrap (swaddle) into may improve listening ability in many children with sensory dysfunction who crave deep pressure.

- The "peanut butter and jelly"—have child lie on mat, then cover with heavy blanket(s) and gently "squish" the child—with even, deep pressure—OT or PT should instruct on usage.

Vestibular dysfunction

- Schedule periods (varying from quite brief to extended) of activities involving motion: swinging, jumping, slide, physio-ball, walking, climbing stairs, see-saw, mini-trampoline, dancing. Periods of these types of activities before a period of quiet listening or working may help to organize the sensory systems so the student will be more able to be calm and focused. They may be part of a "sensory diet" program for a student to help organize and focus the sensory systems.

- OT or PT may place the students on suspended equipment, such as bolster swing, netting swing, four loop (two kids with legs through loops) swing, platform swing, etc.

- PT/OT/teacher may also use equipment such as roller skates, balance beam, scooter board, balance board, etc.

The teacher as detective

It is time to put together the pieces of the puzzle. In order to solve the puzzle, we must put on our detective hats, learn to analyze problematic "situations", and develop *useful* strategies to resolve these situations.

Anytime a difficult situation arises (behavioral, social, academic), the situation must be broken into its component parts and analyzed individually. The first aspect to analyze is the behavior; what does it look like (*describe*)? Next, what happened just before the situation (*pre-behavior situation*)? Then, because this is sensory integration dysfunction we are discussing, we need to know what happened several hours (or days) before (at home, on the bus, at the sitter's last night) that might be related (*never forgets factor*). Finally, we get the *point of view* (POV) of the child who has sensory dysfunction or Asperger's. The POV of this child may be *very* different, distorted or, most likely, narrow, compared to the POV of his or her peers on the same situation.

After getting all the components together, the teacher must *analyze* all of the information to discover the major causal factors. Then it is up to the teacher and the school team to develop a workable *strategy*, and to implement that strategy.

Let's get started! We will look at three case studies—one from a preschool class (Brittney), one from an elementary school (Tyrell), and one from the middle and high school years (Cody).

Preschool class

Brittney is a four-year-old girl, who was a premature baby with a history of frequent upper-respiratory infections. She was described by her teacher as generally pleasant and cooperative in her preschool class. Her teacher and parents are becoming concerned because things are not "coming together" for her. Brittney arrives at school in "slow gear," requiring a lot of attention to get settled in. Her teacher says she is always "several steps behind the rest of the class." It is now May, and her teacher and parents are looking closely at her level of readiness skills for kindergarten.

The absolute first thing we do is ask: "What does the behavior look like?" In other words, *describe* exactly what is meant by "slow gear," "not coming together." If we were strangers walking into the classroom for the first time, what would we see Brittney doing?

DESCRIBE

What does "slow gear" look like?

- Walks in slowly dragging her backpack behind her.

- Affect is flat, does not spontaneously "greet" others.

- Her nose is running and her mouth is slightly open.

What does "several steps behind" look like?

- Wanders around instead of going directly to her cubby when asked.

- Requires assistance getting backpack hung on the cubby coat hook and getting her jacket off.

- Still needs repeated prompts to choose a place to play while other kids arrive.

- Transitions slowly—other kids are already sitting in the group while she is still finishing clearing her area from the previous activity.

What does "not coming together" look like?

- Has a hard time grasping and retaining concepts.

- Does not actively participate in cooperative or group play.

- Is not developing a mature pencil grasp, cannot trace her name without assistance.

- Limited vocabulary, limited use of pronouns, difficult to understand much of the time.

- Still has difficulty playing simple group games.

- Often appears detached and not attending much of the time.

PRE-BEHAVIOR SITUATION

- *Arrival:* Ms. Williams greets the children and takes attendance while the children trickle into the room. Then Ms. Williams reminds the children to put their things in their cubby and choose a place to play.

- Depending on the day, the children will transition to group time about 20–25 minutes after arrival.

- At group time the children participate in either a literacy, science, math, or music and movement activity related to the "theme of the week."

NEVER FORGETS FACTOR

Unidentified at this time due to limitations of her language skills.

POINT OF VIEW (BRITTNEY'S)

- *Arrival:* Brittney indicated that she likes coming to school, likes the toys and likes her friends. "My bag is big. I don't know where my cubby is. It's ok."

- *Transition time:* "Where does this go?"

- *Group time:* "It's fun."

ANALYZE

- *Arrival:* Backpack is heavy—proprioception, muscle tone, strength, endurance
  - *Finding cubby*—Sensory processing of the visual, auditory, motor planning, vestibular? Due to frequent upper-respiratory infections?
  - *Hanging backpack*—Proprioception, motor planning, body awareness
  - *Finding a place to play*—Difficulty prioritizing sensory stimuli—what do I attend to first?—Is the teacher talking to me? Sensory overload—too many choices?
  - *Greetings*—Language delay, difficulty organizing and formulating a response

- *Transition time*—Difficulty prioritizing sensory stimuli, language processing issues

- *Group time*—Proprioceptive, tactile, auditory, visual, vestibular

STRATEGY

After the parent/teacher conference, the parents requested evaluations by the speech therapist, child development specialist, and occupational therapist. Here were the suggested strategies.

- *Arrival:*
  - Visual cues to redirect attention and guide (visual schedule, photo in cubby)
  - Modeling appropriate greetings
  - Provide larger hook for cubby
  - Alerting activity
  - Teacher to limit choices for arrival activity—choice of two. Brittney chooses where she wants to play from two pictures. Teacher prompts her to use "I" statement—"I want to play with the…"

- *Transition time:*
  - Give verbal warnings prior to transition
  - Use of visual timer
  - Break down task
  - Use of transitional song or music (the "clean-up" song)
  - Delineate physical space—where do you sit?

- *Group time:*
  - "Wake up your body activity"
  - Visual cues for redirecting
  - Verbal prompts for redirecting
  - Preferential seating
  - Sitting on "bumpy" side of "Move 'n Sit" cushion
  - Visual schedule
  - Encourage participation/movement

After implementing some of the strategies that had been suggested by the team, Brittney's parents and teacher are encouraged by some recent positive changes. Brittney is now more independent (removing coat, hanging book bag in cubby), is experiencing smoother transitions between activities, and has increased her level of participation in group activities.

Elementary school

Tyrell is a bright child who is driving his 1st grade teacher, Mr. Grady, insane! It seems to be the same issues every day. Tyrell interrupts during morning circle and is constantly talking about carnivorous plants. When the class breaks into groups and travels from center to center, Tyrell is usually off task or complaining that a classmate is "bugging him." Mr. Grady is spending a large portion of his time redirecting Tyrell.

The absolute first thing we do is ask: "What does the behavior look like?" In other words, *describe* exactly what is meant by "off task"; how is Tyrell interrupting? If we were strangers walking into the classroom for the first time, what would we see Tyrell doing?

DESCRIBE

Interrupting looks like:

- sitting on the rug and squirming continuously
- talking without raising his hand when he wants to answer or add something to what Mr. Grady is saying
- distracting the other students by talking to himself out loud.

Center time behavior looks like:

- Tyrell looks like he is lost in a fog:
  ◦ looking all around the room
  ◦ asking many obliquely related questions, then switching rapidly to talking about carnivorous plants before getting an answer to the question he just asked
  ◦ looking at the teacher, the classroom aide, and the clock furtively.
- Tyrell appears to be quite clumsy, getting too close to his classmates or to furniture:
  ◦ he often jostles classmates (unintentionally—then blames them)

o he bumps into desks and chairs and blames the furniture, or the person next to him.

PRE-BEHAVIOR SITUATION

- *Circle:* Mr. Grady conducts daily classroom business—attendance, lunch count, etc., while the class sits at their desks. Then Mr. Grady tells the class to come over to the rug for morning circle.

- *Centers:* Depending on the day (the school follows a six-day cycle), Mr. Grady will start centers between 9:30 and 10:15.

NEVER FORGETS FACTOR

Mr. Grady spoke to Tyrell in an informal way, during a quiet time. He discovered that, for the specific day of the observation, Tyrell's mother cooked oatmeal for breakfast because his little sister wanted it. Tyrell hates oatmeal, it makes him want to throw up. Tyrell ate his usual breakfast of a blueberry muffin and a spoonful of peanut butter. Also, he outgrew his favorite pajamas and his mother is getting him new ones today...what if they don't have dinosaurs on them?

POINT OF VIEW (TYRELL'S)

- *Circle:* "The rug is real itchy. The other kids are always bumping into me or kicking me for no reason. Carnivorous plants are very interesting. You ask questions, don't you expect me to answer?"

- *Centers:* [Heavy sigh] "Centers are too confusing! I never know where I'm supposed to go next. Remember when I was timed out because I didn't know where to go and you said I did? You said that each center would be 10 minutes, but sometimes a center is longer than 20 minutes, or shorter, like only 8 minutes. I never know if I'll finish before you tell us to rotate. Besides, people are always pushing their chairs out right in front of me or standing where I want to stand."

ANALYZE

- *Circle:*
  - The rug is itchy and kids are always bumping into me—Sensory.
  - Carnivorous plants are interesting—Pragmatics.

- *Centers:*
  - ○ Centers are confusing—Sensory-executive functioning.
  - ○ Centers are supposed to be 10 minutes—Inflexibility/pragmatics.
  - ○ People are pushing chairs—Physical proximity/sensory.

STRATEGIES

Mr. Grady enlisted the help of the school speech therapist and special education teacher to help him devise strategies to help Tyrell. Here's what the three of them came up with.

- *Circle:*
  - ○ Cotton bath towel that Tyrell may sit on (washable and portable, too).
  - ○ Decided to let the towel serve as a physical space prompt.
  - ○ Used a laminated circle (red on one side, green on the other) as a stop–go sign—"go" for raising your hand, and "stop" for no interrupting by raising hands or talking out loud.
  - ○ Mr. Grady even had an index card that said "on topic" ready to point to if Tyrell (or anyone else) responded with a completely off-topic remark or story.

- *Centers:*
  - ○ Mr. Grady purchased a timer for the classroom, that showed how much time was left in red.
  - ○ Posted a "rotation schedule" that all of the groups could easily follow.
  - ○ Created a "stay on task" card for Tyrell, which Mr. Grady or the classroom aide could easily and inconspicuously flash to Tyrell (or any other student).
  - ○ Mr. Grady or Mrs. Guiles (the classroom aide) always gave a verbal "one minute warning" before it was time to rotate to the next center.
  - ○ Mr. Grady incorporated carnivorous plants when appropriate.
  - ○ For the bumping issue: the towel or a hula hoop; and social stories about accidental bumping and awareness of personal space.

Mr. Grady and his team were flabbergasted by the results of the strategies they had implemented. Many other children in the class benefited from the changes as well, not just Tyrell. The class was actually running quite smoothly and Mr. Grady was no longer exhausted by 9:15am!

Middle and high school

Cody is a 13-year-old boy who is often sullen and frustrated because he does not seem to "fit in" at school. His teachers are frustrated because Cody is completely disorganized and usually seems to be on the edge of having an angry outburst or a tearful meltdown, even when someone is trying to help him! Cody is smart, but does not work to his academic potential. Cody's teachers schedule a meeting to discuss Cody's problems.

During this meeting, Cody's teachers realize that he is having difficulty in each of his classes with behaviors and not getting homework done or handed in on time.

DESCRIBE

Behaviors look like:

- sullen and unhappy
- becomes angry—slamming books shut, loudly talking to himself
- usually to class late and without the required homework, books, or supplies
- "off task"—staring out the window or just staring into space
- cannot seem to follow simple directions given in class
- anxiety—almost hyperventilating while repeating, "I, I, I just don't understand…I'll never be able to do this…why me?…"

Homework is:

- usually a day late and/or partially completed
- very sloppy—many erasures or scribbled-out portions
- very large and difficult-to-read handwriting
- often not as instructed.

PRE-BEHAVIOR SITUATION

- *Behaviors:* At the beginning of the school year, each teacher established rules about the behaviors expected in his or her classroom.

- *Homework:* At the beginning of the school year, each teacher made clear her or his expectations and rules about homework assignments.

NEVER FORGETS FACTOR

Cody's teaching team selected one member, Mrs. Lopez, Cody's science teacher, to talk with him about "his day" on one specific day. Cody spoke quietly and was near tears. Mrs. Lopez was surprised at how Cody worried about getting on the right bus after school, because a classmate, Lon, made fun of Cody in the 5th grade for absentmindedly getting on the wrong bus. Cody is also worried that some of the "wild boys" will lock him in his locker and he will die of asphyxiation. Also, too many bad grades will prevent him from getting a scholarship to a good four-year college.

POINT OF VIEW (CODY'S)

- *Behaviors:* What am I supposed to do? All of my teachers are out to get me. I never can do anything right. Slamming a book shut is a lot better than punching someone (which is what I wish I could do). I can never hear the teacher, there is always someone else talking or ripping paper from a notebook or tapping a pen. How can I concentrate with all of those distractions? When I think about karate, my favorite thing in the whole world, all of the noise goes away and I can imagine myself doing a form or a flying side kick! Then, all of a sudden it is time to go, and the teacher is talking about homework in a really fast voice and he knows I'll never get it finished because it is always too much …then what about getting into a good college?

- *Homework:* I never know how long the homework is going to take to do. Sometimes I don't get the assignment written down or I lose it in my locker or somewhere. I get home and my mom wants me to do the homework, but I get confused about how to do it. Sometimes I get really mad because I lug all these huge books home and somehow I don't have the right ones! Then everyone nags me because my writing is "illegible." My hand hurts from writing and it still looks terrible. Even when I get my homework done and handed in on time, I still make mistakes on it and get it back with corrections.

ANALYZE

- *Behaviors:*
    - Disorganized—Executive functioning.
    - Difficulty understanding/interpreting directions—Pragmatics.
    - Difficulty understanding/interpreting direction—Sensory.
    - Anxiety issues.

- *Homework:*
    - Organization—Executive functioning.
    - Difficulty understanding/interpreting directions—Pragmatics.
    - Difficulty writing out assignments—Sensory/pragmatics.
    - Anxiety issues.
    - Difficulty coping with feedback—Pragmatics.

STRATEGIES

Cody's team of teachers got together with a special education teacher and an occupational therapist. After brainstorming, here are the strategies the team came up with:

- *Homework:*
    - Color-code all books and folders according to subject area (science book has red cover, science notebook is red, science folder is red).
    - Make sure Cody writes down all assignments (at first, have teacher, paraprofessional write down assignments—gradually make Cody responsible for writing in agenda).
    - Reduce the amount of homework, for example by just doing odd-numbered questions.
    - Discuss possibility of using computer to type some homework, to alleviate writing problem.

- ○ Have paraprofessional, teacher, or older student(s) "anchor" at the end of the day to help Cody go over agenda and gather correct homework supplies.
- ○ At home, have a permanent "study area" set up and ready—a place with few distractions, yet easily accessible to parents for help.
- ○ Graph paper to line up math problems.
- ○ Timer—work for 15 minutes, then three-minute break.

- *At school:*
  - ○ An adult "anchor" that Cody meets with at the beginning of every day to make sure that things are running smoothly, homework was completed, quickly review his schedule for the day, etc.
  - ○ Have adult assist with initial organization of locker and color-coded subject areas.
  - ○ Color-coded checklist of needed materials (science, social studies, and gym clothes for the morning).
  - ○ Allow Cody to stay at locker a couple of minutes longer to use checklist for supplies.
  - ○ Preferential seating in classes.
  - ○ Prearranged signal that allows Cody one or two minutes of quiet, unobtrusive "break time" when he becomes overwhelmed and feels like lashing out or crying.
  - ○ Encourage Cody to practice breathing techniques when experiencing stress or anxiety.
  - ○ At the end of the day, "anchor person" helps Cody create a visual schedule for the next day, including any known substitutes, assemblies or other changes in the schedule.

By the middle and high school years, a student who has Asperger's or sensory dysfunction is likely to be plagued by depression and riddled with anxiety. It becomes critical for such a student to have an adult "anchor," with whom they "touch base" at the beginning and end of each school day.

Cody's teachers were reluctant at first to put time into scheduling the things that Cody should be doing independently by now, such as writing in his agenda and making out his own daily schedule, plus taking the time to meet with him at the beginning and end of school. However, the teachers agreed to a trial run, and appointed a paraprofessional as the "anchor" person.

By the end of the trial period, Cody was much less sullen and almost always had his homework completed, and in on time. His emotional meltdowns were much less frequent, and his parents reported that homework time was no longer a daily battle of wills.

Behavior as a means of communication

Behavior, behavior, behavior. More importantly, what is the child telling us? It is our experience that behavior is perhaps the most powerful means of communication a child possesses. For children with sensory issues (to full-blown sensory integration dysfunction) behavior is often misinterpreted or misunderstood, and as a result, the situation seldom improves, frequently resulting in a vicious cycle or a power struggle. It is our assertion that if you (as parents, teachers, therapists, etc.) become more aware of the intent of the behavior, it might become easier to develop more effective/successful behavioral strategies.

POTENTIALLY CHALLENGING BEHAVIORS

- Perseveration
- Physical proximity issues
- High/low activity level
- Emotional lability
- Distractibility
- Low frustration level
- "Shut down"
- Runners and hiders
- Non-compliance
- Aggression (physical, verbal)

Now, because it is our assertion that many times it is the sensory issues/needs that drive the behavior, it makes sense to begin to tease apart challenging behaviors using a sensory-based perspective. Again, the senses and the sensory systems do not work in isolation. So, generally speaking, you will need to consider more than one system or sense when analyzing behavior.

POSSIBLE COMBINATIONS AND PERMUTATIONS

- Perseveration—Craving/aversion of a specific sensory input (tactile, visual, vestibular, auditory, proprioceptive, gustatory, olfactory)

- Physical proximity issues—A consistent need to be too close (in another person's "space") or a consistent need to maintain an inappropriately far distance (tactile, proprioceptive)

- "Hyper" activity level—Children who get "revved" up quickly and have a lot of energy, but the energy tends to be diffused (visual, auditory, vestibular, tactile, difficulty prioritizing stimuli)

- "Hypo" activity level—Takes a long time to get "revved" up, appears to lack energy, what energy they do have tends to be diffused (visual, auditory, vestibular, tactile, difficulty registering stimuli)

- Emotional lability—A child who vacillates emotionally—laughing one minute, sobbing the next (sensory processing, sensory overload—unable to regulate)

- Distractibility—Shifting focus frequently and abruptly, attention is fleeting (difficulty prioritizing stimuli in all senses and sensory systems)

- Low frustration level—Easily frustrated (motor planning, delayed skill development for specific activity, sensory overload)

- "Shut down"—Refusal or inability to respond (sensory overload)

- Runners and hiders—Children who bolt, leave, exit an area without permission; children who hide—when it is not a game of "hide-and go-seek"! (seeking a certain type of sensory experience, avoiding a certain type of sensory experience)

- Non-compliance—Resisting or refusing to respond to a task or activity (an aversion to a specific sensory experience, or inability (actual or perceived) to perform task)

- Aggression—Physical violence or the threat of physical violence (sensory overload, perceived threat, actual or perceived inability to perform task)

Home/school partnerships

It is our belief as well as our experience that effective communication is the absolute cornerstone of effective home/school partnerships. This is the only way that you can have a truly win-win-win (parents, school, and, most importantly, the child) situation. We are keenly aware, both as teachers and as parents, that truly effective communication requires at least willing participants. In other words, if the parents are not fully participating or the school is not fully participating then "everyone is not at the table."

In the Perfect World...

- the home and the school intentionally, quickly, build a positive rapport

- the family is well-informed and respectful of the child's school life

- school personnel are well-informed and respectful of the child's home life

- communication between home and school is as frequent as is needed and is thoughtfully sent and thoughtfully received

- home and school both have enough time and resources to share victories and positive experiences

- parent–teacher conferences (phone or in person) are occurring and they are constructive and collaborative

- everyone is on "the same page" and mutually supportive of goals.

Some questions...possible solutions...?

- *Is everyone committed to building positive rapport?*—Are there participants who are talking "down" to others, using jargon, or whose communication (verbal or nonverbal) might be construed as negative or demeaning?

- *Does the family have a true understanding how their child's program functions?*—Has the family been given information, in their primary language, explaining their child's program(s) in terms they can understand?

- *Do the school personnel have a basic idea of how things function at home?*—Has the school been given appropriate, pertinent information to aid the school in understanding the child's situation?

- *Are there limitations at home or at school? If so, are all parties informed?*—Is it a family situation that could affect the child's education program? Is it a school situation that could affect the child's education program?

- *Are you acknowledging the other parties' efforts?*—As the family are you taking the opportunity to note and to appreciate the effort being made by the school on behalf of your child? As the school personnel, are you taking the opportunity to note and to appreciate the effort being made by the family on behalf of the child?

Creating a plan

Effective communication can occur in several different ways. We have found that creating a plan using focused questions will usually be a great help to the child with sensory dysfunction. Of course, the obvious first choice is that the home and school collaborate by answering these questions and devising a strategy separately or by scheduling a time to develop the plan together. For a variety of reasons, this may not always be possible. A form that can be used at home or in school might include the following:

- child's name

- address

- date of birth

- diagnosis

- sensory profile

- resources available (people, equipment, time, and money)

- areas of strength

- areas of difficulty (list in order of priority)

- what is already working (strategies, incentives, etc.)
- what specifically do you want to see changed or improved? (behavior, skill development, social interactions, self-care skills, etc.)
- who/what do you need to access? (additional resources needed)
- strategy to address target behavior from a sensory perspective
- a record of how strategy is working
- whether to continue/discontinue strategy.

Developing a student/child portfolio

Another, more comprehensive way to communicate and share information home to school, school to home, or during transitional situations, whatever those could be, is to put together a portfolio. An outline of the information contained in such a portfolio is presented on the following pages (pp.102–8). This portfolio is most commonly used in preschool and early elementary settings. It is time-consuming and you do need to know the child well.

Adapting to the child

We view the senses, and sensory systems, with regard to learning, as individual building blocks of differing sizes and shapes that fit together to build a strong foundation. It is our view that this could look like a country-style stone wall where you are grabbing stones from the field and fitting them together as best you can to build a solid wall. For some individuals, this "developmental wall" comes together effortlessly and naturally over the course of their early years. For others, this "wall" takes a lot a work and ranges from unsteady to already shifting, beginning to show gaps, and crumbling. The blocks are the senses, the sensory systems, skill development, learning, and behavior. For some individuals the senses and sensory systems work well cooperatively to help, seemingly effortlessly, develop and support age-appropriate skill development, learning, and behavior. For other individuals, the senses and sensory systems do not work well cooperatively, which may result in developmental delays, learning difficulties, and behavioral problems.

Basic Child Information

Child's name

Nickname

Current address

Phone #

Birthday

Parents, "significant people"

Siblings

Pets

Allergies—food, medication, etc.

Food preferences/aversions

Diagnosis, if any

Pertinent previous medical and/or sensory history

Prior and current related services, if any

Communication Abilities

Alternative/augmentative forms of communication (examples: sign language, visuals as language supports, picture exchange communication system, etc.)

Strategies for communication that work for this child (examples: pause before repeating a question, using a quiet voice to gain attention)

Intelligibility—what helps support child's ability to be understood? (examples: cues to slow down, cues such as "bite your lip" for the letter "F")

Motor Needs/Adaptations

Adaptive equipment child may need (examples: special seating, slant board, loop scissors, special pencil grasp)

Helpful hints (examples: reminding child to hold rail on stairs, placement in line, type of movement that child seeks, movement child avoids—climbing, crawling, swinging, "crashing," jumping, etc.)

Does the child have a "sensory diet"? If so, what was included in it? (examples: brushing program, spinning program, weighted vest, weighted lap belt, suspension equipment, taking regular breaks from classroom)

Adapted from Handicapped Children's Association, Inc. portfolio guidelines
Copyright © Polly Godwin Emmons and Liz McKendy Anderson 2005

Classroom Management

Reinforcers—What is reinforcing to this child? (examples: encouragement and praise, time doing a favorite activity)

Relaxers—What relaxes this child? (examples: looking quietly at a book, squeezing playdough, deep pressure activities such as jumping, "pushing against the wall," getting a "bear hug," listening to music with headphones on)

Transition times—How is this child during transition times? If transition is difficult, what was helpful to use? (examples: five-minute, three-minute, one-minute auditory warning, use of a visual timer, visual schedule to see what is coming next, a picture of what is coming next to hold)

Behavior management—Did this child have a specific behavior management plan to address challenging behaviors? If so, what were some of the challenging behaviors? How were these handled in the classroom? (examples: planned ignoring, reward system, clear and consistent consequences)

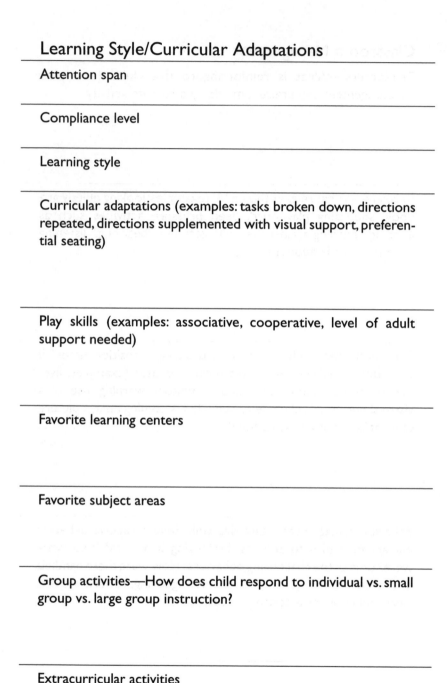

Learning Style/Curricular Adaptations

Attention span

Compliance level

Learning style

Curricular adaptations (examples: tasks broken down, directions repeated, directions supplemented with visual support, preferential seating)

Play skills (examples: associative, cooperative, level of adult support needed)

Favorite learning centers

Favorite subject areas

Group activities—How does child respond to individual vs. small group vs. large group instruction?

Extracurricular activities

Adapted from Handicapped Children's Association, Inc. portfolio guidelines
Copyright © Polly Godwin Emmons and Liz McKendy Anderson 2005

Work Samples

Art work (self-portrait, "free" art, paintings etc.)

Writing sample

Cutting sample

Photos of child in home or school setting

Abbreviated Secondary School Form

Student's name

Student's age

Student's date of birth

Classification/diagnosis

Prior placement

Prior services/accommodations/modifications

What works—academic

What works—behavioral

What does not work—academic

What does not work—behavioral

Areas of high interest/hobbies/sports/clubs

Getting "ready to learn"

It is our experience as teachers that one cannot work on the assumption that all children come to your classroom or activity "ready to learn." This can be for a variety of reasons (illness, fatigue, family issues, etc.), but we are going to look at the possible sensory components to attain that optimal "quiet alert" state in order to be ready to learn. The challenge is that some children will arrive that are over-stimulated (you know, the students who are buzzing around the room and may need to be peeled off the ceiling), while other students will arrive under-stimulated and under-aroused (yawning, head resting on hand, "sleeping with eyes open"). It is our stance that whether you teach preschoolers or secondary students, it may be well worth your time to develop a (literally) one-minute routine that will help to improve focus and better organize your students' sensory systems to achieve that "quiet alert" state. This routine can be strategically utilized prior to starting an activity/lesson, during an activity/lesson, or after an activity/lesson as a transition to the next thing. You know your students best! You know when they need a break or need to reorganize, regroup or refocus. We are suggesting that you review your daily routines from a more sensory-based perspective—accessing the sensory systems to facilitate that "quiet alert" state. After incorporating a more sensory-based approach, we are confident that it will prove beneficial for your entire classroom…your students and yourself!

This routine can and should look different, depending on many factors, including, for example, age level, the type of activity that you are going to be engaging in, time of day, and time of year.

Let's say you are a preschool teacher and have a great science activity planned for circle time. You are just coming out of snack and beginning to gather the kids on the rug. It is now October, so you can easily anticipate that four kids will be over-stimulated by the transition from snack clean up, three will not be sure that circle comes after snack every day (wandering), three will be tired/lethargic and generally under-aroused and not have started to "perk up" yet. Here is a routine (after your regular transition song/movement/music activity) that might work for your classroom.

- As kids gather, let them know that it's "time to wake up our bodies" and get ready to learn.
- Wake up your eyes…get them ready to look (rubbing temples).

- Wake up your ears…get them ready to listen (massage ears).

- Wake up your nose…get ready to smell (touch nose, crinkle nose).

- Wake up your brain…get ready to think (scalp massage).

- Wake up your cheeks, chin, eyebrows, elbows, ankles, etc. (by rubbing or rolling or bending).

- Reach up high and stretch…feel your shoulders and stretch your arms (posture awareness).

- Stretch out your legs…point and flex feet and toes (body awareness).

- Pat your arms…give them a rub, then a pat (body awareness).

- Take three deep breaths, roll your neck.

- Now we are ready to learn.

You will know day to day, how and when it needs to be tweaked a little bit and changed to meet the ever-changing sensory needs of your students.

You are a 3rd grade teacher and you are transitioning your class from a reading lesson to math lesson. Today we will (each day stretch breaks look a little different but still only take about one minute):

- jump in place three times

- reach to the ceiling then to the floor three times

- close our eyes, think about the number "5" and take five deep breaths (in through your nose, out through your mouth).

You are a secondary social studies teacher and are getting ready to hand out the dreaded essay test! You tell the class that they have 45 seconds to "stretch and move." Ask them to

- take three deep breaths

- gather their thoughts.

Then (at teacher discretion) pass out gum, pretzels, or lollipops at the beginning of the test—sensory input for improved attention/organization.

As you can see, the teacher-facilitated sensory and transition components decrease dramatically as the student ages. The student is expected to develop the skills and self-awareness that are necessary to achieve and maintain that "quiet alert" state for optimal teaching and learning. Through awareness and practice, most students will develop the ability to self-monitor. Self-monitoring doesn't necessarily happen because a student hits a certain age or grade. Therefore, if you have a student, whether preschool, elementary, or secondary, who is having academic or social difficulties, ask whether the student's self-awareness or self-monitoring skills are age-appropriate. If the answer is "no," could it be that the student has not developed the sensory/sensory-processing abilities to be successful? So, basically what we are suggesting is to "think out of the box" and don't be afraid to try some new sensory strategies!

Modifying teaching and the curriculum

Before we look at specifically modifying the curriculum for a child with sensory issues or sensory dysfunction, we feel it is important to take a look at the overall developmental appropriateness of the program. This is particularly important in early childhood programs such as daycare settings, toddler class, preschool class, Universal Pre-K program, early elementary school program or a before- or after-school program.

By developmentally appropriate program we mean a learning environment and activities that are based on knowledge of "typical" development of children within the age range you are serving...remember that developmental timeline? The research we have seen indicates that most children who progress within a range of slightly above or slightly below their chronological age are still considered to be "typically" developing. Therefore, a "developmentally appropriate program" should be one modified to a child's unique level and range of development in all areas. However, we do recognize that there are children whose developmental age may be significantly below their chronological age where a "developmentally appropriate program" may need considerably more individualizing or adapting.

The good news is that many teachers are modifying the curriculum already. But you may want to look a little more closely at your lesson plans, the daily routine, and the classroom environment, whether you are a preschool teacher, elementary school teacher, or secondary teacher. More good news, it has been our experience that including sensory strategies may benefit most, if not all, students. Let's begin by taking at look at modifying lesson plans.

The following steps will look very familiar to most teachers:

- Step 1: Select the skill or subject area to be taught.
- Step 2: Identify the specific skill or topic to be taught.
- Step 3: Identify the curricular goal/objective.
- Step 4: Create and develop a plan for instructional delivery.

In virtually every classroom, there are students who have difficulty participating or completing a lesson. Many times, these difficulties can be boiled down to sensory/sensory-processing issues. As a teacher, you have already put a great deal of effort into creating a dynamic, purposeful, engaging lesson/activity. We are suggesting that you now take a look at this thoughtful lesson plan and consciously be aware of the sensory components...if it includes oral direction giving and/or lecture (auditory), writing on the board/overhead/powerpoint/handing out written instructions (visual), if there is a hands-on element or a manipulation of something (kinesthetic), or if it involves numerical concepts/computation (math)...you get the idea. Chances are, there are some kids in your classroom who have difficulty with learning, comprehending, or processing. Typically there are also students in the class who present with behavioral challenges who may, or may not, have learning difficulties. So, what we are trying to illustrate is that:

- there are children with behavioral challenges, but no apparent learning difficulties
- there are children with learning difficulties, but no apparent behavioral challenges
- there are children with behavioral challenges and learning difficulties
- there are children who have no apparent behavioral challenges or learning difficulties.

As teachers we would like to order 25 students from the fourth category for the next school year, please!

What we are going to address next are some curriculum adaptations that can be used to support students who present with behavioral challenges, learning difficulties, or both. We want to make it clear at this point that we are not suggesting that a teacher who has already worked hard to create a very good lesson plan go back to the drawing board and create multiple lessons to address the same objectives (we know how much time that would take!). What we are suggesting is that there are strategies to help you "get more bang for your planning buck!"

The following are some suggestions for additional ways to modify or adapt the curriculum for a child with sensory dysfunction.

- Time—consider adapting the time allotted for learning and task completion.

- Size—consider adapting the number of items the child is expected to learn or to complete.

- Level of support—if possible, increase the amount of assistance given to this child.

- Participation—consider adapting the extent to which the learner must be actively involved in the task.

AN EXAMPLE OF AN EARLY CHILDHOOD LESSON PLAN

The following is an example of how you can develop and implement a lesson by incorporating sensory strategies to better meet the needs of your students.

Objective: At the end of this lesson, the student will be able to retell a simple story.

Here are some ways in which you may already be developing a lesson for this objective.

- Gather the kids in a circle, read the story and ask follow-up questions.

- Choose a book that has repetition built into it.

- Utilize an over-sized book that incorporates textures and bright colors.

- Encourage students to participate verbally during reading.

- Encourage students to participate through both words and movement.

Now you can analyze how the children in your class participated/reacted to this activity.

You may have a child(ren) in your group who:

- just wanted to shout

- just wanted to stand there jumping (not appearing to listen)

- frequently crawled across the circle (over their neighbors) to feel the textures in the book

- got a little "lost" or appeared to be daydreaming

- got too excited and started poking, prodding, or pushing their neighbors.

From a sensory standpoint here are few thoughts.

For the "shouter" (possible auditory, impulsivity from sensory load):

- Prepare the whole class, reminding them (*auditory*) to use an "inside voice" during the participation part of the story—practice once or twice (*oral/motor*).

- Use nonverbal prompts such as gesturing "quietly" with exaggerated facial expression (*visual*).

- Give nonverbal visual feedback—wink, thumbs up, etc. (*visual*).

For the "jumper" (possible proprioceptive, vestibular):

- Incorporate some type of music and movement activity as a transition to the reading activity (*proprioceptive, auditory*).

- Prepare and practice for "appropriate" participation (*proprioceptive*).

In our experience, kids who are moving excessively and frantically are not easily able to respond to nonverbal/verbal cues, let alone attend to what you want them to attend to. So, this is where you anticipate this response from this child; you do your best to plan for it.

- Have the child wear a weighted vest (with OT/PT consult).

- Delineate space (tape, towel, rug, hula hoop).

- Give the child something to squeeze (stress balls).

- Teach the child ahead of time a modified "jump"—bending the knees in place of a full jump (remember, it is about adaptive responses—sensory input will stimulate another sensory response).

For the "toucher" (tactile):

- Make the child aware that there are different textures in the book and that everyone will get a turn to touch after the story is finished (*auditory*).

- Give them something textured to hold while reading the story.

- Give visual reminders—stay on your "mat."

For the "dreamer" (visual, auditory, or sensory overload):

- Use the classroom FM system (*auditory*).

- Use auditory trainer (*auditory*).

- Give a verbal prompt paired with a sign to redirect attention to book (*auditory, visual*).

- Arrange preferential seating (near teacher) (*proximity—access to all systems*).

- Provide additional prompts (*physical, visual, auditory*).

For the "poker" (auditory, visual, proprioceptive):

- You need to prepare every single time—when we listen to a story, where do we need to be looking, who do we need to be listening to, where do our hands need to be?" (*auditory, visual*).

- Create spatial awareness, delineate spatial boundaries (*proprioceptive, visual*).

- Use fidget toys (*tactile, proprioceptive, visual, olfactory*).

- Arrange preferential seating on the end, in the back, slightly behind.

- Use voice inflection—keep "reeling them back in"—(Oh boy, look what happens now!).

This is by no means an exhaustive list. There are many other sensory-based strategies that you can implement, and may already be implementing. The point here is to analyze what you are already doing, recognize the sensory components, and start using them to your advantage...now you are beginning to get the "bigger bang for your planning/management/learning buck" that we mentioned earlier!

Chapter 5

At Home and at School: Looking at Strategies

We've devoted a good portion of this book to recognizing and understanding the very complex nature of sensory integration and sensory dysfunction. It is our experience that many children with sensory issues or sensory dysfunction tend to be emotionally labile, easily frustrated, and frequently exhibit behaviors that could be considered immature for their age. We recognize that being a child with sensory issues or sensory dysfunction is often not easy, and can be very isolating. And we understand that being the family member, the daycare provider, or the teacher of a child with sensory issues may not be any easier. It is our experience that developing an understanding and a willingness to try different strategies is often very helpful.

Management techniques

One of the most important areas is communication with the child with sensory issues. Here are some strategies that we have found helpful.

- Gain your child's attention and make sure he or she is listening before giving directions.

- Turn down/off the TV or CD player, or ask others talking to pause before giving your child directions.

- Squat or bend down and ask your child to look at you to make sure you have his or her attention before speaking.

- Use natural gestures as visual cues, such as pointing or motioning when you give your child directions.

- Be sure to speak slowly and clearly.

- Have your child repeat the directions back to you.

- Repeat directions as needed.

- Choose words carefully—only use words your child understands and keep the message short and simple.

- Have realistic expectations for your child—while chronologically your child should be able to follow multi-step directions, developmentally your child may simply not be ready.

We believe that most children have a strong sense of wanting to "belong" and "do a good job." Many parents, teachers, and other adults who are unfamiliar with the concept of sensory issues or sensory integration dysfunction may misinterpret a child's challenging behavior and react negatively. In many cases this can lead to power struggles over a behavior that is misconstrued as "defiant," "non-compliant," or "attention-seeking." That is not to say that children with sensory issues or sensory integration dysfunction never exhibit "typical" behaviors—they do! But it is our experience that frequently their "challenging" behaviors tend to be sensory-driven.

Some of the behaviors sometimes seen in children with sensory issues and sensory integration dysfunction that are frequently overlooked or misunderstood are self-calming behaviors. Some of these self-calming behaviors may include:

- stroking

- rocking

- mouthing objects

- kinesthetic movement

- humming/mouth noises

- visual self-stimulation

- leaning up against things/seeking deep pressure

- staring into space.

Since behavior is a means of communication, children with sensory issues and sensory integration dysfunction who are exhibiting self-calming behaviors are, most likely, trying to tell you something—"I am trying to organize my sensory systems!" Sometimes, parents and teachers, with the best of intentions, try to get the child to stop a self-calming behavior. For example, a parent has a child who is humming constantly and no one in the family can hear the television. The parent may insist the child stop humming only to hear the child begin seconds later making a different mouth noise. Or take the 4th grade teacher who has a student staring out the window in a fixed gaze watching the trees blowing in the wind—the teacher may decide to close the blinds to make the student stop and refocus on the lesson, only to find the student then staring in a fixed gaze on the classroom clock's second hand. Or how about the parent whose child is mouthing on his shirt sleeve? The parent insists the child stop because it is ruining the shirt; the child briefly stops chewing on the shirt, but then begins chewing on the highlighter his sister left on the counter while doing her homework. Or take the preschool teacher whose student is leaning so hard into the shoulder of the child sitting next to her at circle time that the child complains that it hurts—the teacher reminds all of the children to sit up nice and tall with eyes on the book, only to then see the child slowly scooch backwards until she is across the room leaning against a bookshelf.

Bottom line, if a child with sensory issues or sensory integration dysfunction is exhibiting a behavior that appears to be self-calming, and that behavior is stopped, the child will most likely replace it with another, yet similar, self-calming behavior. If the child is not allowed to do so because the behavior is determined to be inappropriate or unsafe by an adult, the child may have difficulty staying "organized" or calm, which may result in an even more challenging, inappropriate, or unsafe behavior.

Helpful behavioral strategies

While prevention of challenging behaviors through a multi-sensory approach is often best, the following are some behavioral strategies you may want to try that we have found helpful.

REDIRECTION/"SWITCHING GEARS"

Encourage the child to engage in a more socially appropriate use of an object or a behavioral alternative. For example, when a preschool-age child becomes upset because his brother is sitting so close to him that his arm touches his (tactile defensiveness), becomes upset and begins throwing the blocks, say to the child, "Blocks are for building. Let's build with the blocks," while helping the child physically distance from his peer so that their arms are no longer touching. Or, if you are in Burger King and your child is refusing to stay seated (sensory overload) you may want to consider taking your child (and your food) and heading out to the car or a quieter spot to eat.

MODELING A DESIRED BEHAVIOR/"DO AS I DO"

Here you demonstrate the behavior you would like the child to engage in. For example, a parent might say to a young child, "Please put your dirty dish in the sink," while the parent is putting his or her dirty dish in the sink. Or if you are feeling incredibly frustrated you could say something like: "I am so upset right now I could just scream…but, I am going to calm myself down, take three deep breaths, and regroup."

REINFORCING A MODEL

You could reinforce the behavior of another child who is engaging in the behavior you would like the child to engage in. For example, you are going to the store and you see a mother with two children entering, and both of the children are nicely holding hands with the mother. You can just point out to your children: "Look at those kids, they are holding their mom's hands. That's a safe way to walk through the parking lot. Wow, so when we walk in the store, I want us to hold hands and be safe too."

"IF, THEN" STATEMENTS

These are statements that restate a naturally occurring, positive event to prompt increased compliance. For example, a parent is trying to get a child ready to go to an appointment. The child is refusing to get dressed and beginning to tantrum. The parent prompts the child by saying: "If you get dressed and we can get downstairs quickly, then you can have your breakfast sooner. Or, for the older child who is having difficulty finishing the math homework: "If you finish your math homework, then you may take a break."

STOPPING THE BEHAVIOR BEFORE IT STARTS

Prior to the child reacting with inappropriate behavior, the adult can prompt the child toward a behavior that is more socially appropriate. For example, a kindergartener is obviously frustrated trying to fit a peg into the pegboard. The teacher may say: "Ask for help."

RIGHTING A "WRONG"

Following an incident where a child has demonstrated some inappropriate behavior, thrown something, wrecked his work or another child's work, pushed furniture aside, etc., allow him or her some time to calm down. Then help the child to find a way to make the situation better—put something back, redo it, fix it, etc.

TAKING A BREAK

When a child is beginning to tantrum, and you determine that the source of the impending meltdown is sensory related, calmly remove the child or the object from the immediate environment to reduce or eliminate the sensory offense. If you are unable to do this, at least validate for the child that you know this sensory input is very difficult for him or her to tolerate. For example, a teacher has observed that one of her 3rd graders has an overly sensitive sense of hearing and that his desk is very close to the electric pencil sharper. The teacher also observes that every time someone sharpens a pencil, this student yells. The teacher may decide either to move the child to another desk or to move the electric pencil sharpener. This same student might be on a field trip to a science museum where the docent shows the class a certain machine by turning it on—it is very loud. The teacher is unable to move the child away from the machine due to the number of students in a small physical exhibit space, but discreetly bends down and whispers in the child's ear: "I know this is hard for you to listen to."

RESPONSE PREVENTION—PHYSICAL PROXIMITY

This involves placing yourself near the child to serve as a prompt/reminder for the child to maintain an expected behavior. For example, a 1st grade teacher moves a child's chair or desk physically closer to the teacher so that he can more easily prompt the child to maintain the expected behavior. This can be helpful with the student with sensory issues or sensory integration dysfunction because the closer the eye the teacher has on the child the more likely he or she is to observe sensory-based patterns of behavior and so address them.

Unhelpful behavioral strategies

The following are some behavioral strategies that, in our experience, are not helpful for a child with sensory issues or sensory integration dysfunction.

PLANNED IGNORING

This behavioral strategy is also sometimes called "extinction." When the inappropriate behavior occurs, the parent or teacher does nothing, says nothing about the behavior, and acts as though it never happened. In theory, a child's behavior that is not given attention will eventually stop occurring. If the behavior is the result of a sensory issue or sensory integration dysfunction, planned ignoring will be, at best, ineffective.

"TIME OUT"

This usually refers to the child being removed by an adult from a desired activity for a period of time due to inappropriate behavior. If the behavior is a result of a sensory issue or sensory integration dysfunction, the child may fight the time out both verbally and, often, physically, in order to be able to seek the desired sensory behavior. When this happens, a "small" inappropriate behavior (pushing by a peer to get to a toy or activity) may become a "large" inappropriate behavior (swearing at or purposefully pushing the teacher, or both).

EXPRESSION OF DISPLEASURE

Here the parent or teacher lets the child know that he or she is disappointed with the child's inappropriate behavior. Unfortunately, while it is not supposed to be used, an angry tone often accompanies this behavioral strategy. Many children with challenging behaviors resulting from sensory issues or sensory integration dysfunction are not "choosing" the behavior, rather they are driven to it by sensory needs or deficits. An adult (especially one with whom the child feels connected) who expresses displeasure or becomes angry may only make the child feel more anxious, resulting in the child being even less able to cope with sensory input.

NONVERBAL CONSEQUENCES

Following a child's inappropriate behaviors, a parent or teacher may sometimes give the child nonverbal feedback such as a slight shaking of the head or another mild expression of disappointment which may be too subtle for the child to notice. When the behavior is associated with sensory issues, as is often the case for a child with an autism spectrum disorder, the feedback will probably be lost. However, other children (perhaps with learning difficulties and/or a mental health component) may have a heightened emotional reactivity to facial expressions and nonverbal cues, perhaps as a result of emotional lability, the child may over-react to the expressed displeasure by becoming "unglued," yelling back, running away, etc.

PHYSICALLY BLOCKING OR CONTAINING

This refers to the blocking of a behavior or holding a child to stop a behavior that could be dangerous to the child or others. In our opinion, this behavioral strategy should only be used as a last resort when serious harm to the child or another could occur. For the child with sensory issues or sensory integration dysfunction this type of blocking or restraint may only result in the behavior escalating.

Preventive behavioral strategies

If you are looking to try to prevent as many inappropriate behaviors from occurring as possible, it is important to understand why they may be happening in the first place. Unfortunately many parents and teachers of a child with sensory issues or sensory integration dysfunction, and other adults with whom the child may come into contact, have no idea why the child is "misbehaving" and may even ask him or her "Why did you do that?" Trust us, there is always a reason for "misbehaving" and the child usually doesn't have a clue why he or she did something.

We think it is important to mention that as you begin implementing different behavior strategies, remember to look for and acknowledge the feedback you will get through the child's arousal state. This may include changes in a child's emotional state, appearance (eye contact, skin tone, excitement level) or behavior (aggression, regression).

Considering and modifying the environment

Before we look at ways in which the environment can be modified or adapted for a child with sensory issues, it is important to identify what factors can be inherently arousing or calming. *Inherently arousing factors* include:

- loud, sudden noises and/or voices

- strong odor(s)

- fast movement/unexpected movement

- bright lights, bright colors
- light or unexpected touch
- changes in temperature
- background stimulation/noise
- unpredictable events.

Inherently calming factors include:

- soft voice
- soft odor(s)
- steady, expected movement such as rocking
- low lights, natural light, muted colors
- even temperature
- minimal background stimulation/noise
- predictable structure and routine.

Whether it is at home, daycare, school, or any other environment where a child with sensory issues will spend time, it is important to take a look at the environment. While it is not realistic to attempt to modify every aspect of the environment for a child's sensory integration dysfunction, most times a little additional awareness can go a long way. Sometimes, just some simple changes in a home, school, or daycare environment can have a very beneficial effect for the child. Here are some questions that may provide a helpful foundation when assessing an environment.

- *Level of stimulation*—Is the level of stimulation too much or too little for the child's sensory systems?

- *Level of structure and routine*—Is there enough consistency and predictability? Is there too much?

- *Number of sensory activities*—Are there enough sensory activities? Is there a variety of sensory activities? Are there so many choices it is confusing or over-stimulating?

- *Types of colors*—Are the colors bright? Are they muted? More importantly, do they match the level of arousal of the child? A child who has a low level of arousal may respond to bright colors and become more alert, while a child who is over-stimulated may respond to muted colors and become more calm.

- *Type of lighting*—Are the lights fluorescent? Are the lights low-watt lamps? Is it natural lighting? Is it dark? Is it bright sunlight? Ask yourself, is the type of lighting a good match for this child's sensory systems?

- *Type of music*—If there is music, is it loud? Is it soft? Is it "heavy metal," "soft rock," "rap," "classical," or "new age"? How are the child's sensory systems responding to it? Some children with a high level of arousal may respond to "new age" music or "nature" sounds by calming. Some children with a low level of arousal may respond to louder, faster music by becoming more alert.

- *Use of textures*—What types of textures are in the environment? (Consider carpets, furniture, etc.) How is the child responding to them?

- *Noise*—Is there an area where this child can go to have some "quiet time" if needed? What is the level of noise—if it is too loud for this child, can something be turned down? Are some type of ear plugs or ear protectors appropriate?

- *Types of aromas*—What scents do you smell? How many scents do you smell?

- *Number of transitions*—Is this an environment that requires the child to transition from one activity to another? If so, how frequently? How is the child prepared for any transitions? Are the current methods of transitioning working? If so, identify what they are so they can possibly be used in another setting. If not, why not? What modifications or accommodations might be helpful for this child during transitions?

- *Accessibility of adaptive equipment*—If the child uses any adaptive sensory equipment as part of a "sensory diet," is it available in this environment? Is it available whenever it might be needed or only at certain times? What equipment needs to be brought in to modify this environment to help this child to be more successful?

- *Awareness*—Are the people in this environment aware of the child's unique sensory needs? If not, be clear on your reasons why. If so, be clear on your reasons why. Are your reasons, whatever they are, the most beneficial for the child? Do the people in this environment have a clear understanding of any modifications or adaptations this child may need? If so, are they kept current? If not, is there a need to identify resources—written or otherwise?

It is our experience that it is often easier to modify or adapt the environment for a child with sensory integration dysfunction during the early years. There is no doubt in our minds that "necessity is the mother of all invention." For us, both as parents of children with sensory needs and as teachers, the times when things are really not working well are often the times when we are most open to trying something different. The following are some suggestions or strategies you may want to try either in your home or in your classroom.

- *Visual barriers*—Use furniture to provide visual barriers to help delineate where one area or activity needs to end and where another area or activity may begin. For example, if there is a toy that needs to stay in one area, such as the trucks staying in the block area, then consider positioning the block shelf to help create a visual barrier.

- *Visual cues*—Use tape or some other marker to help delineate where a child is supposed to be. For example, ribbon can be tied onto the side of the grocery cart to give the child a visual cue as to where he or she is expected to hold on to the cart. Or tape can be used in a classroom to give children a visual cue as to where to line up to leave the classroom. Many young children, especially those with poor body awareness, may not know where to be if asked to "come sit in a circle" or "line up at the door."

- *Aroma therapy*—There are many different ways to do aroma therapy—lotions, plug-in scents, etc. that are now available in a variety of scents in many stores. We have found vanilla to be calming, lemon to be alerting…for mothers and teachers as well as kids! Check it out!

- *Visual supports*—Labels, pictures, picture schedules, social stories all provide visual support to understanding language. These can be very helpful for a child who is not certain what something is, what it is used for, what is happening next, etc.

- *Predictable routine*—Create as much of a predictable and consistent routine whenever possible...not rigid...just predictable. Notify a child in advance of changes and keep visual support on hand as needed.

Be prepared to take a break or leave the environment if necessary. Our experience is that once a child with sensory integration dysfunction becomes anxious, agitated, or upset as the stress level increases, the language abilities often decrease making it very difficult to "talk through" a situation or "talk down" the stress level. Sometimes the child just needs to take a break from the environment.

Another useful suggestion is to create a "sensory bag" or "sensory basket" that can go from environment to environment with the child...home to daycare...to school...to Grandma's...to wherever! The idea is that if the child starts to lose composure due to sensory input or overload, the "sensory bag" can be accessed to use a sensory approach to help manage the arousal state or behaviors. While each child's "bag" should be based on his or her individual sensory needs, here are some suggestions that may help you get started:

- something to squeeze—stress balls, etc.
- two footprints that can be put on the floor for jumping or stomping
- lotion with one of the more calming scents, such as vanilla
- two handprints that can be placed on a wall as a deep pressure "push place"
- a washcloth or small towel to wipe off anger
- a write-on, wipe-off board and dry erase markers
- an unbreakable mirror so the child can see his or her emotions
- words or pictures to help the child begin to identify these emotions
- a visual or auditory timer to guide a child to continue to use the sensory activities until calmer
- an oral/motor blow toy (like a whistle) with any ability to make sound removed.

Whether you are a parent, daycare provider, or teacher of a child with sensory integration issues, this sensory approach to behavior management can be extremely effective. Our experience has been that while initially children may need to be directed to use the sensory bag, they will soon be open to it as a suggestion and may quickly gravitate toward using it independently. Why? Because it makes them feel better and helps them regain composure using a positive, proactive approach. The other aspect of the sensory bag that is extremely valuable is that it will give those working or living with the child valuable "clues" as to which sensory activities help the child to calm and regroup. For example, if the child often chooses to blow on the oral/motor toy then taking five deep breaths may work well as a calming tool. Or if the child often chooses a deep pressure activity such as "pushing the wall" or jumping or stomping on the footprints, then this may be a child who responds well to heavy work as a calming tool.

Self-care strategies

For many children with sensory issues or sensory dysfunction, self-care skills may range from challenging to aversive. Some children will have a heightened sensitivity to sensory input; for others, it may be a decreased awareness of sensory input. The following suggestions may be helpful.

Bathing/showering

- An unbreakable mirror (with suction cups on back) to attach to side of tub so child can "see" self while washing, shampooing, and rinsing. The child is then able to anticipate when he will be touched/lathered/scrubbed/rinsed.

- Consider allowing the child to do as much of the lathering/scrubbing/rinsing as possible (this gives her a greater sense of predictability and control).

- Be aware of water depth (gravitational insecurity).

- Consider purchasing and applying an inflatable faucet cover to avoid injuries, even if your child is older (poor body awareness).

- Make sure that you are real clear about the temperature regulation (some kids will want to be "polar bears", others may be in danger of being scalded) (lack of temperature awareness).

- Consider the level of stimulation—amount of toys, noise level, number of people in the bathing area (over-stimulation).

- Consider covering the bottom of the tub/shower with a rubberized anti-slip mat (coordination issues).

- Provide verbal prompts as needed to support independent bathing/showering (difficulties with motor planning).

- Washcloth over eyes when shampooing/rinsing.

- Soap on a rope/hand mitts (hand dexterity).

Toothbrushing

- Try different textures and flavors of toothpaste.

- Try different toothbrush shapes, kinds, sizes.

- May need desensitization prior to brushing.

- Parental follow-up may be needed even for older children.

- A water pick instead of flossing.

Dressing

- Consider elastic-waisted pants (tactile, motor planning).

- Try to be flexible with clothing choices—there may be a sensory sensitivity behind them.

- You may need to provide assistance with dressing for a longer than expected period of time (fine motor, motor planning, etc.).

- For some children too many choices may be overwhelming.

- Remove tags.

- Buy seamless clothes.

- Some children may prefer long-sleeved or short-sleeved shirts, short or long pants regardless of season or may have difficulty changing wardrobe from one season to the next.

Food

- Be aware of food temperature (may need food reheated or cooled down).
- Be aware of texture preferences and aversions.
- Take into account any heightened awareness/lack of awareness of flavor.
- Allow for difficulty with manipulating eating utensils (use weighted utensils, utensils with different grips, drip-proof/spill-proof bowls, etc.).
- Consider the visual presentation of food (colors, shapes, touching).
- Plan ahead—think about what types of food and drinks will be offered and consider possible substitutions.
- Keep in mind food may need to be cut up more, given in smaller amounts.
- Monitor consumption—some children will not feel full, some may not feel hungry or thirsty.
- Use verbal prompts for chewing, wiping face, etc.

Bedtime

- Have a consistent bedtime routine.
- Try calming music.
- Try different lighting.
- Use weighted blankets.
- Experiment with different pajamas—styles and fabrics.
- Allow time for reading/journaling.
- Have things set out for the next day.

These are just some suggestions which you might find helpful. We have found by sharing with others (parents, teachers, daycare providers, etc.) you will discover additional strategies to try out and expand your list.

Chapter 6

More About Asperger's Syndrome

Recently, there has been a significant increase in the diagnosis of autism spectrum disorders, especially Asperger's syndrome. This is becoming of particular consequence to the educational community and to teachers in general education as well as in special education classrooms. The average age of diagnosis for Asperger's syndrome is currently six and a half years. This means that for most children, a diagnosis may not occur until the child has been through preschool and is into elementary school. Frequently, it is the pragmatic issues (taking turns in conversation, voice modulation, interrupting, physical proximity, perseverating on a topic, etc.) and the sensory issues that create the "red flags" for parents (and teachers) to seek out a diagnosis for the child. Children with Asperger's do not "outgrow" their odd and quirky behaviors—which are frequently sensory driven.

The purpose of this chapter is to explain Asperger's syndrome in a down-to-earth and easy-to-understand manner. Dealing with this enigmatic disability on a day-to-day basis is a frustrating and daunting task. In the interest of being efficient and practical, the rote, technical (impossible to understand) definitions will be given first. In order to facilitate understanding, the traditional definitions will be followed by examples and brief explanations. It is also intended to provide practical, effective strategies that may be helpful for many children with sensory issues or sensory dysfunction.

Diagnosing Asperger's from the DSM-IV: Selecting from the menu

Okay, take a deep, cleansing breath and uncross your eyes. And if you understood any or all of the DSM-IV definition in Chapter 3, then either you are a developmental pediatrician specializing in pervasive developmental disorders, the parent of a child with Asperger's syndrome, or much too interested in medical terminology.

It is important to keep in mind as you read through this section of the book, that Asperger's syndrome is truly part of a spectrum disorder; that is to say that the symptoms can range from very mild to very severe. And, to add to the confusion, the different symptoms within the same child may vary significantly. For instance, a child may have almost normal eye contact (mild gaze avert), but have an extremely narrow range of interests—he will only talk about dinosaurs. Or a child may have the vocabulary of an adult, but not be able to comprehend basic directions and instructions given by a teacher or parent.

Now we are ready to tackle each of the diagnostic criteria individually, keeping in mind that each child is an individual and may exhibit characteristics anywhere along the spectrum, from mild to severe. Also, the diagnosis of Asperger's syndrome is a *clinical diagnosis*, that is to say that the doctor (psychologist, neurologist) looks at the list of clinical characteristics and determines if the child has the symptoms, characteristics, and behaviors that match. There is no biological marker or blood test to determine if a child has Asperger's syndrome (or most of the autism spectrum disorders). The sections that follow here correspond to the full text of the diagnostic criteria set out in Chapter 3.

Qualitative impairment in social interaction
IMPAIRMENT IN THE USE OF MULTIPLE NONVERBAL BEHAVIORS

A child, Dan, is sitting in the classroom, looking at a book. Another child, Kate, comes over and asks, "What book are you looking at?" Dan does not respond, appearing to be engrossed in his book. Kate continues, "Dan, can I look at the book with you?" At this point, Dan, without looking up, says, "Ok." Kate proceeds to sit down next to Dan.

Kate then asks Dan if she can hold the book for a while. Dan hands the book to Kate. Kate opens the book, placing half of the book on her knee, and the other half on Dan's knee. Kate browses the pictures and reads the text. But as she does so, she glances furtively over toward Dan, asking, "Are you ready for the page to be turned yet?"

In response to Kate's question, Dan grabs the book and turns to the back of the book, stating, without looking directly at Kate, "This is my favorite page; it has the most question marks on it. I like question marks."

Overtly, this may be an exchange that teachers, particularly preschool and early elementary teachers, witness on a regular basis. Dan is acting aloof, but seemingly within the boundaries of what would be considered developmentally appropriate. However, if we analyze this exchange, a pattern begins to be revealed.

Let's look at the nonverbal social interactions from this scenario. Kate is "reading" the nonverbal cues. Dan seems engrossed in a book so she asks to join him. She looks over to Dan for clues that he may be ready to move to the next page; when she does not get any nonverbal feedback, such as Dan looking over to her, or away from the page, Kate finally asks Dan.

Conversely, Dan appears to totally disregard most of Kate's nonverbal cues. Notice that Dan did not even acknowledge Kate (verbally or through body language) when she sat down next to him. Then, when Kate asks to read the book with him, Dan responds by wordlessly shoving the book into Kate's hands. Additionally, instead of turning to the next page, Dan simply flips to his "favorite" page and expects Kate to be enthusiastic about the shape of question marks. Children with Asperger's are masters of the "non-sequitor"!

FAILURE TO DEVELOP PEER RELATIONSHIPS APPROPRIATE TO DEVELOPMENTAL LEVEL

It is lunchtime in a nondescript elementary school. All the 5th graders troop to one table to eat, the 4th graders to the next table, and so on. At the 5th grade table, the boys sit at one end, eating quickly and dividing themselves into teams, so they can play football with Mr. Hutchinson as soon as they get to the playground. However, one child, Dustin, is sitting in the middle of the fray eating and talking to the monitor about his science project.

The bell signaling recess rings, and a happy, energetic throng quickly streams out of the cafeteria and onto the playground. As usual, a group of 2nd and 3rd grade children begin a game of tag. The 4th grade girls jump rope, while the 4th grade boys play football. The 5th grade girls join in the jump rope game or roam the playground in groups, giggling, laughing, and watching the boys play football. The one notable exception to the daily playground rituals is Dustin, the 5th grader, who refuses to play football with the other boys, but instead happily plays tag with the 3rd graders.

This is one of the hallmarks of the Asperger's child: tending to get along well with adults, but preferring to "play" by himself, or with children who are much younger. Any of the "typical" 5th grade boys would be mortified to be caught playing tag with the 3rd graders or to spend their lunch conversing with the monitor! These are the kids that just don't seem to have real friends: peers that want to come over to play, and who are, in turn, invited to the friend's house to play. Often what happens is that the parent becomes worried when the child has "friend" after "friend" over, only to find out that none of these friends wants to return for a second time. Frequently, the child who has Asperger's (and the parents) is left devastated and frustrated. The bottom line here is that the child has difficulty developing and maintaining meaningful, reciprocal friendships.

LACK OF SPONTANEOUS SEEKING TO SHARE ENJOYMENT, INTERESTS, OR ACHIEVEMENTS WITH OTHER PEOPLE

The entire kindergarten class was mesmerized. Choruses of "ooing" and "ahhing" were punctuated by shrieks of delight as the children watched the magician perform the opening portion of his act. The teacher noticed that all of the children pointed in unison when the magician asked where the colorful flowers had disappeared to, or when the dove flew into the hat. All of the children, that is, except David. A little taken aback, the teacher stopped and thought for a moment; David never really seemed to point, even when he wanted something! All year the classroom aide had joked that her arms had lengthened by three inches from David's constant tugging and pulling to show her things. In this instance, David is not interested in sharing the group's excitement about the magician, but may demonstrate excitement when a classoom guest discusses a topic that is more closely aligned to David's personal interests.

As with any of the characteristics of Asperger's, the manifestation can range from mild to extreme. On the mild side for this characteristic, is the child who seems very pleased with her accomplishments or finished projects, but appears to lack enthusiasm for showing her work to others (even her teacher or parents). This often leads the adults to view the child as "shy" or lacking in self-confidence. On the extreme end is the child who rarely points to a desired object, but instead will stand in front of the sink if he wants a drink of water, or walk over and stand beneath the letter "A" if that is the answer to the teacher's question.

LACK OF SOCIAL OR EMOTIONAL RECIPROCITY

James is a bright, attractive 2nd grader. He is beyond himself with excitement because today a classmate, Steven, is coming over to play. James has been eagerly anticipating Steven's arrival, making sure that all of his action figures are properly laid out on his bedroom floor. Finally the doorbell rings! James, smiling broadly, grabs Steven by the arm and starts pulling him toward his bedroom, chattering anxiously about his action figures.

Steven happily plays with James and his action figures for over 45 minutes. Then Steven asks James if he has any other toys or games. James nods toward a huge toy chest and shelves. Steven goes over to the toy box and finds a very cool Lego set.

"Hey, James, let's build a haunted house!"

James shakes his head, "No."

"Okay, then how about we race your remote control car?" Again, a very uninterested James says no.

"How about Nintendo?" queries Steven.

Finally, Steven gives up and trudges down the hall to James's mom. "I think I want to go home now. James only wants to play with his action figures."

James's mom quickly calls James over and tries to cajole him into playing some other games. "Honey, Steven is your guest and he wants to play something else for a little while. James, how would you feel if you visited Steven and he only wanted to play with his Nintendo? Come on, James, it will be *fun* to play a different game for a short time."

Steven leaves while James remains happily in his room, playing with his action figures.

In this example, James is like most other children his age in many respects. He is very excited about having a classmate over for a play date and he wants to play *his* favorite game first. However, it is his inability to comprehend emotional or social reciprocity that makes James stand out. While it is normal for a child this age to not have a complete handle on the idea of sharing and reciprocating, James's actions and responses are too rigid. By this age, most children are able to understand basic manners and polite sharing. In this situation, it is evident that, even though James desperately wanted Steven to come over and play, James does not comprehend the rudimentary elements of turn taking, and is not able to understand Steven's perspective at all.

These are the students in the classroom that may appear to have a unique sense of "justice" which is driven by their egocentrism. As far as they are concerned, it would be perfectly acceptable for them to be "line leader" or "messenger" every day; but it would not be "fair" if another child were "line leader" or "messenger" every day.

Restricted, repetitive, and stereotyped patterns of behavior, interests, and activities

For a diagnosis of Asperger's, this needs to be manifested by at least one of the following:

- encompassing preoccupation with one or more stereotyped and restricted patterns of interest that is abnormal either in intensity or focus

- apparently inflexible adherence to specific, nonfunctional routines or rituals

- stereotyped and repetitive motor mannerisms

- persistent preoccupation with parts of objects.

We want to emphasize here that although only one of the aforementioned attributes is needed as part of the criteria for diagnosing Asperger's syndrome, many children with Asperger's will present with *more* than one of these characteristics. And again, this is a spectrum disorder, so while one child will present as "always and intensely" a certain way, others may present as "behaving that way at times."

Roberto is a bright and energetic six-year-old. He is also the resident expert on dinosaurs at Little Elms Elementary School. Roberto impresses most of the children and all the adults in the building with his in-depth and comprehensive knowledge of dinosaurs. Virtually all of Roberto's clothing and school gear are dinosaur themed, right down to his underwear and socks! In fact, Roberto is so excited about dinosaurs that he able to focus on little else. All of his conversations quickly revert to dinosaurs, and he becomes visibly upset when asked to talk about something else. What was at first an endearing trait rapidly lost its allure as Roberto's teacher and classmates hear the same facts about dinosaurs, over and over again, on a daily basis.

Many young children are interested in dinosaurs (or trucks or Thomas the Tank Engine), but children with Apserger's often differ in the *quality* and intensity of their focus. Like Roberto, the "topic of interest" typically does not lead to reciprocal conversational exchanges. The child is repeating facts, regardless of whether it is an appropriate time to relate such information or whether the people around him care to hear the information.

Tariq is a 3rd grade student who daydreams and appears to be quite anxious about ridiculously mundane aspects of the class schedule. Every day, Tariq asks if his mother is going to pick him up from school or if he is going to ride the bus home. Tariq has ridden the bus home from school every day since the first day of school; once and only once has his mother picked him up for an early dental appointment. The teacher has come to the conclusion that Tariq is truly upset until he hears an adult tell him that he is, indeed, riding the bus home after school today. Tariq also becomes unduly agitated if the class does not leave for physical education, art, or lunch at *exactly* the time they are supposed to leave; if art is at 10:45, then leaving at 10:47 will most likely cause Tariq to cry or start his "worry fingers" (clasping and unclasping his fingers into fists, as if he is squeezing an imaginary tennis ball). The teacher often wonders if Tariq receives enough attention at home from adults, or if he gets too much attention and is babied.

In this example, Tariq is genuinely disturbed by the most subtle changes in his routine and is quite inflexible about time and scheduling. He appears to be in an anxiety and adherence-to-routine loop with his daily preoccupation with how he is going to get home.

Terrance is a handsome and placid 1st grader. In fact, Terrance is so "laid back" that the chaos at recess and free play never seems to bother him. Terrance can usually be found in a corner, or even amidst the fray, lining up his matchbox cars and concentrating on watching the wheels spin. Sometimes, Terrance sits at the computer and presses the same button over and over again—he loves to see the cat jump over the mouse!

Many children in the 1st grade, particularly the boys, will play with cars or "movable" toys whenever they are given "free choice." Likewise, children tend to relish time at the classroom computer. However, it is the quality and duration of Terrance's "play" that make it significant. Terrance is preoccupied with a part of an intended play object or learning tool. He is not playing together with other children or attempting more sophisticated (or even different) play activities.

Clinically significant impairments in social, occupational, or other important areas of functioning

In all of the aforementioned examples, the children are viewed by their peers as social misfits—or at the very least, socially very odd. Children with Asperger's generally want friendships, but do not have the social skills or social savvy to create and maintain a friendship. Frequently, children with Asperger's are very socially immature, socially aloof, or downright little dictators. Typically, students with Asperger's are not easily integrated into peer groups and present with social (and behavioral) challenges when the class is required to participate in cooperative group activities. The student with Asperger's will lack the social and communication skills to work easily or effectively in peer group situations.

No clinically significant general delay in language

When Kwang was three years old, his grandfather gave him the nickname, "Professor Kwang" after demanding a "citrus fruit and a protein" for a snack. Soon the whole family began referring to Kwang as "PK." PK's vocabulary was amazing. His preschool teacher marveled at his ability to tell adults about his intricate fantasy world. However, by the time PK was in 6th grade, his parents and teachers were exasperated and perplexed by his inability to hold a reciprocal conversation with his peers. PK was certainly still a "little professor" with an extensive vocabulary and a voracious appetite for comic books, but he constantly interrupted, talked off topic and never actually listened to, or looked at, the speaker!

PK is a very familiar example of a child with Asperger's, who, when he is young, dazzles people with his vocabulary and intelligence, but as he grows older his difficulties initiating and holding a conversation (the pragmatics of language) become increasingly more pronounced, leaving him socially isolated.

No other clinically significant developmental delays

Jevon had always been described as bright, but a little bit "odd." He walked early, talked early, and was able to feed himself and dress himself as well as any other child his age. Now, at the age of ten, Jevon is a "dreamer" who excels at video games and swimming. He loves going on vacations to the beach with his family, as long as he has his stash of Chips Ahoy cookies and his Game Boy with him. Jevon can certainly be described as emotionally and socially immature, but doesn't that describe a lot of boys his age?

Now, this is why we refer to Asperger's syndrome as a "package deal." A child (or adult) who has Asperger's is not defined by a single attribute, but rather by an inventory of behaviors and characteristics that must be assessed as to how (qualitatively) they combine to affect the child (or adult). However, to have a bonafide diagnosis of Asperger's syndrome, a child must have at least average cognitive abilities (though many children with Asperger's fall into the "gifted" range of cognitive abilities).

No diagnosis of another pervasive developmental disorder or schizophrenia

A certified developmental pediatrician, child psychiatrist, child psychologist, pediatric neurologist, or general pediatrician must have extensive developmental background information, as well as an in-person interview, to assess whether a child has Asperger's syndrome and to rule out other autism spectrum disorders and other conditions that may manifest similar characteristics or behaviors. Again, we must emphasize that Asperger's syndrome is a "package deal," so the child must actually been seen *in person* by the professional rendering the diagnosis.

Social and communication deficits: Pragmatics made easy

Pragmatics are the cornerstone of our social "language" and the key to understanding the deficits in communication that children with Asperger's syndrome experience. It is essential for every parent and every teacher to have a basic understanding of the components of pragmatics because pragmatic difficulties appear to be the common, rogue thread running through the core areas of impaired social skills and a lack of meaningful, reciprocal communication. Simply put, understanding pragmatics will give a parent or a school professional the foundation upon which to devise concrete strategies to help the child with Asperger's *function more easily* and with much less frustration in school, at home, and out in the community.

It is important to note here that one of the defining characteristics of a child with Asperger's syndrome is that he or she will possess *superficially normal language.* That is precisely why it is so important to understand the subtleties of "social language" and communication. However, one caveat here:

this section divides pragmatic speech into discrete component parts and discusses each part individually, in isolation from the rest. In reality, of course, all of the component parts occur simultaneously to produce the "real" pragmatics of speech. We will now look at the following components of social communication in turn:

- pedantic language
- difficulty taking turns
- interrupting conversations
- difficulty with voice modulation
- odd prosody
- inappropriate or absent voice inflections
- difficulty staying on topic and responding appropriately
- difficulty with facial cues and body language
- gaze avert
- narrow range of interests
- literal interpretations
- difficulty generalizing information
- physical proximity issues.

Pedantic language

Pedantic language is what most of us consider to be the "little professor" vocabulary and grammar. Children with Asperger's will often use big vocabulary words and very formal sentence structure and end up sounding like "mini-adults" instead of children.

The average five- or six-year-old might say that he wanted a cookie when asked what he wanted from the bakery. A five- or six-year-old with Asperger's might say something like, "I'd prefer a cake-like confection." I once overheard a group of 4th grade boys bragging about how fast each could run: "I'm the fastest runner here!" the first boy proclaimed. "Are not, I'm way faster than you," chimed in the other three boys, simultaneously. As the four boys volleyed "are not" and "are so" back and forth a few times, a classmate, who had been standing near the group, playing with a video game, said loudly,

"Jenna is the student in our class who is most fleet of foot. However, Mike L. is the swiftest runner in the entire 4th grade."

A typical middle school student might say that the kids in his class "acted badly for the substitute, goofing around, not listening and talking too much." A middle school student who has Asperger's might say, "the students took advantage of the substitute today, most of them were behaving obnoxiously; talking back, making irritating noises and being very noncompliant."

Many children have extensive vocabularies, but will not engage in such formal usage in daily situations. Of course most of the typical children in the previous examples knew what the big vocabulary words meant, and quite likely use such formal language structure and vocabulary when writing school assignments, but would not speak like that in front of their peers—it would be too weird and adult-like!

Difficulty taking turns

Difficulty taking turns in conversations is by no means a trait reserved exclusively for a child who has Asperger's. Many children, particularly younger children, seem to take a little while to get the hang of taking turns in a conversation, just like it takes time and maturity to learn to take turns while playing a game. However, a child who has Asperger's will not naturally mature into a reciprocal conversationalist, the same way that a typical child will.

The students in every 1st grade classroom spend a great deal of time learning the art and science of turn taking. Turn taking is woven into every activity throughout the day. First graders learn to take turns speaking, using toys, playing games, completing work, eating, using the restroom, being "first," asking questions and lining up. However, by the time children are in the upper elementary and middle school grades, most are relatively self-regulating as far as turn taking is concerned. Most conversational exchanges inside the classroom, in the cafeteria, on the bus, in the hallways, and on the playground are free flowing and don't require a referee to keep track of whose turn it is to speak—the rules of conversational turn taking have, in essence, become internalized.

Interrupting conversations

Interrupting conversations is a hallmark of the child with Asperger's. As with the turn-taking protocols that most typical children learn to internalize, the "don't interrupt" rule seems to be very difficult for the child with Asperger's to grasp and master. Again, most typical children will learn "interruption" etiquette rapidly as they grow through each school year. For example, most kindergarteners (at the beginning of the school year) will interrupt anyone at anytime. Yet, by the end of the school year, most kindergarteners know to raise their hand and wait to be called on and *not* to interrupt a classmate or adult who is speaking unless it is something very important (like the principal is entering the room or the hamster got out of her cage). By the late elementary grades, most students will become annoyed with a classmate who constantly interrupts or inappropriately speaks out of turn. However, a middle school student who has Asperger's is very likely to interrupt constantly and inappropriately, seeming much more like a considerably younger student.

Difficulty with voice modulation

Voice modulation difficulties tend to be quite obvious, and, for the most part, very irritating. Again, most typical children will learn quickly that they need to adjust their voices to "match" the situation at home or at school. For example, in school a quiet voice is used for library and testing situations. There is absolutely no talking or noise making during a fire drill, a loud voice is usually fine on the playground during recess, and each teacher will tolerate a certain noise level in the classroom during group projects and transition times. At home, shouting may be allowed while playing outside, but never at the dinner table or while someone is sleeping. And, just like in the classroom, each household has a noise level that is acceptable for various family activities, such as watching television or playing a board game.

Unlike their typical peers, children with Asperger's may have great difficulty being able to adjust voice decibel levels to "match" the activity that they are currently engaged in. Most of us know a child who only has two voice levels: "loud" and "off" or "barely audible" and "off."

Odd prosody

Prosody is basically the rhythm, pitch, and tempo of a voice. While each person has a voice that is as unique as fingerprints, many children with Asperger's will have a very odd or strange prosody in their voices. Typically, a child with odd prosody may have a voice described as a high-pitched "sing-song" voice, a monotone voice, a computer-generated voice or a cartoon-like voice. Often a child with Asperger's will have such a strange or offbeat cadence that it may seem as if he or she is speaking with a foreign accent.

Inappropriate or absent voice inflections

Voice inflections while reading and speaking are essential to give meaning to what is being said. Consider these sentences and how the meaning and intent of the sentence changes when a different word is emphasized.

- *He* said you took the car.
- He *said* you took the car.
- He said *you* took the car.
- He said you *took* the car.
- He said you took the *car*.

As children learn to speak, and then read, they learn to raise the pitch of the voice at the end of a question (whether reading or talking conversationally). This raise in pitch tells the listener that it was a question and not a statement or an exclamation.

It is virtually impossible to discuss inflection without including prosody in the discussion. Most typical children already have conversational inflections (as opposed to reading) mastered by the time they enter school. A child with Asperger's who speaks in a monotone or sing-song voice and whose voice inflections are either absent or inappropriate, will have a hard time getting others to understand the *intent* of his or her words. Right now, go back a couple of paragraphs and reread, aloud, in a monotone or sing-song voice, that same sentence *without* emphasis or inflection. What a nightmare for the listener and for the speaker—What did you mean to say? What were you attempting to communicate? How is the listener going to interpret what you just said? You were using all of the correct words, in the correct order for meaning—why all the confusion?

Difficulty staying on topic and responding appropriately

Difficulty staying on topic occurs, in varying degrees, to most preschool and early elementary children. The art of staying on topic increases rapidly as children are exposed to the social etiquette and structure of a school day (during reading circle, we talk about the book the teacher is reading, not about our cat throwing up last night). By the time typical children enter the late elementary grades, they will be conversationally "on topic" most of the time inside and outside of school. Certainly by middle school, they will find the person who is off topic in conversations to be odd. Middle school is also the time when many children become aware of the time-honored manipulation of *intentionally* encouraging a teacher to "go off topic" onto a tangent, so that material will not be covered and an assignment or test may be delayed!

A child with Asperger's will almost always have difficulty staying on topic, or at least *responding appropriately to the content of the conversation.* Whether or not a child remains "on topic" is quite obvious to the listener; responding appropriately to a topic can be more of a qualitative issue. A typical child in 3rd grade might talk about her aquarium when the class is discussing a science unit dealing with animal habitats. An aquarium would certainly be considered a habitat for her pet fish. However, a 3rd grader who has Asperger's (and an intense interest in bacteria) might talk about how high humidity affects bacteria growth in the Amazon rain forest.

Difficulty with facial cues and body language

Difficulty recognizing and responding to the facial cues and body language of others is a major stumbling block in understanding the social world around you—at home, at school, and out in the community. Typical toddlers understand the basic facial expressions of the people around them—they know by looking at Dad's face and hearing Dad's tone of voice whether Dad is happy, sad or mad. A kindergartener might offer a hug to a friend who is frowning and tearing up. Most 1st graders certainly know when a teacher lifts her index finger to her mouth and says "shhhhh," then folds her arms across her chest, that the class needs to quiet down right now!

In contrast, an 11-year-old who has Asperger's may be completely oblivious to (or confused by) facial expressions and other body language: unable to differentiate between a frown and a grimace; unable to decipher the body language that would warn a typical peer that the teacher is about 30 seconds away from giving the whole class detention, so now would not be a good time to complain about the kid sitting behind you touching your chair with his feet.

A teenager who has Asperger's would most certainly be overwhelmed and confused by the rituals and nuances of flirting, dating, and "socializing." Such an inability to correctly read body language and facial cues often leads to an intense sense of frustration, depression, and anxiety. All too frequently, teenagers with Asperger's become socially isolated and potentially suicidal.

Gaze avert

Gaze avert has a very wide range of dysfunction, from very mild gaze avert to complete gaze avert and everything in between, including intermittent gaze avert and situational gaze avert. A child of any age with Asperger's may not even face the person whom he is addressing, let alone look that person in the eye. A student with Asperger's may have wonderful eye contact when she is answering a math problem, but may have very noticeable gaze avert during transition times.

A typical child learns quickly that you need to look at the person you are speaking to, and, conversely, that people look at you when they speak to you. Parents and teachers will often watch for degree of gaze avert when attempting to unravel the cause of a disagreement or fight ("Johnny, look at me. Did you call Dan a name?"). A child who has Asperger's may or may not look, regardless of guilt or innocence in such a situation.

Narrow range of interests

Narrow range of topics of interest is another hallmark of Asperger's syndrome. Again, this is a qualitative issue. Typical children of all ages may become enamored with a sport, hobby, cartoon character, or theme (e.g., trucks, Barbie dolls, dinosaurs). The three- through six-year-old set is particularly notorious for taking on a character or a theme and spending a large amount of time somehow involved with the specific theme. Many girls and boys seven through teenage years become very interested in a specific sport or hobby or musical group. Most of us can remember the phases (as our parents referred to them) we went through growing up… "Your brother just lived and breathed for Little League baseball and the New York Mets," "Remember that summer that you learned to play the guitar? You spent every waking moment playing that thing!"

On the other hand, the area of interest for a child with Asperger's takes on a whole different quality and intensity than that of a "passing phase." Sure, my brother, at nine, could give you all the names and statistics of the entire Mets roster, but he was also able to hold conversations that did not revolve around, or revert back to baseball. My brother was also interested in doing other things, too. He certainly loved baseball, but an opportunity to go swim at the local pool or go to a movie was never turned down. In fact, his best friend did not share a love of baseball, but they remained best friends, always talking about and doing other things in which they shared a common interest.

A nine-year-old with Asperger's and an intense interest in baseball will have a wholly different tone and intensity for the subject. For a child with Asperger's, virtually all conversations would revolve around or go immediately off topic to the subject of baseball. Baseball would be watched constantly, talked about exclusively, and thought about incessantly. The same baseball-related facts would be repeated time and time again. It would be very difficult to convince the child to engage in other activities.

Nevertheless, children with Asperger's frequently do change areas of interest as they grow older. For example, Polly's son started out at age two with an intense interest in garbage trucks and heavy equipment, at about the age of four he became obsessed with Thomas the Tank Engine, then at age six, his only interest was Batman, then at age nine, he was consumed by an interest in Ninjas and learning the Japanese language. Now, at thirteen, he is trying desperately to fit in with his peers, so he has learned the rules and statistics involved with the National League Football, and learned the lyrics to several heavy metal rock songs. (I questioned him about the songs and he was very clueless about the meaning of the lyrics, but stated tearfully, "All the kids in my grade know these songs and I look like a geek if I don't.") He has learned about these topics to fit in better with his peer group, not because of an intense interest of his own. My son's true obsession now is a specific video game and Jackie Chan, but he is aware that his peers consider too much an interest in these topics to be weird or geeky.

Literal interpretations

The literal interpretation of conversations and written materials is very problematic for children of all ages who have Asperger's syndrome, as are idioms and figures of speech. A typical seven-year-old knows that the expression "it's raining cats and dogs" means that it is raining heavily. A seven-year-old who has Asperger's is likely to look out the window and expect to see cats and dogs falling from the clouds. Likewise, a ten-year-old who hears his father say, "I'm so mad I could spit nails," would realize that his father was expressing his anger. A ten-year-old who has Asperger's would most likely step back and wait for the nails to fly out of his dad's mouth.

A child with Asperger's lives in a very concrete world, where words mean what they mean; implied meanings, figurative language, idioms, clichés, and abstract concepts are not easily recognized or readily understood. Many children with Asperger's are quite good at understanding literal language and deriving factual meaning from what they read. We call it the *"Dragnet Factor"*—"Give me the facts, ma'am; just the facts." Most children who have Asperger's will, from a very early age, repeat rote facts ad nauseam. A 2nd grader who has Asperger's will, most likely, be able to answer any factual question about a story they have just finished reading. However, the moment the questions (about the same story) become interpretive and require inferencing and critical thinking strategies, the student who has Asperger's will be close to clueless. For example:

Andy jumped up and down, pounding his fists on the table. "Cake NOW," Andy yelled as he threw the plate of vegetables on the floor.

Q1:   What did Andy want?
A1:   Cake.

Q2:   How was Andy feeling? How do you know?
A2:   Mad, because he was jumping up and down, pounding his fists and yelling—things people do when they are mad.

A typical 2nd grader would be able to answer both questions, giving appropriate reasons for the response. On the other hand, a 2nd grader with Asperger's would be able to answer the first, factual, question—Andy wanted cake. But the second question would be much more difficult. The most likely response would be—Andy *felt* like he wanted cake, but not his vegetables. Because the sentence did not come right out and say that Andy was mad, interpreting the information in order to come to that conclusion is a very complex and difficult task for a child who has Asperger's.

Difficulty generalizing information

Difficulty generalizing information or process from one situation to another is also a hard task for a child with Asperger's. A typical eight-year-old will be very comfortable ordering food from a McDonald's or a Burger King or a Wendy's. However, even though the process of ordering food at a fast food restaurant is virtually the same for each restaurant, an eight-year-old with Asperger's might not be able to generalize that process from one restaurant to another. Each fast food restaurant looks different, has different names for the meals (and combinations of meals, as my son has pointed out to me), and the employees wear different uniforms. How many times has a teacher heard from a parent that her child can do a task at home "without help," while the child is unable to perform the same task at school (or vice versa)? For a child who has Asperger's, getting dressed, eating, ordering food, or doing a worksheet may not generalize easily from one environment to another. This may often give the erroneous impression that the child is simply willful and noncompliant—"He can do it (dress, order food, complete a task, etc.) when he wants to, but if I ask him to do it (at home, at school, at Grandma's etc.)…"

Physical proximity issues

All children have an invisible "comfort zone" that surrounds them. Typically, younger children tend to be less aware of each other's "space" and may unwittingly infringe upon a classmate's physical comfort zone ("Mrs. Smith, Bradley is too close to me again! His foot is touching mine!"). As they grow, children rapidly become aware of the "rules of conversation." One of these rules is that a person does not stand on top of a classmate, or get directly into a friend's face when conversing with that person.

However, a child who has Asperger's may not only violate this rule when talking to others (too close, too far, facing away), but may have a set of distorted rules concerning his or her own personal comfort zone. Every teacher has had a child who cannot keep his hands to himself in line, but will tearfully proclaim that classmates are "pushing" and "hitting" him when he has not been touched! Many a parent of a child who has Asperger's has dreaded the long ride to Grandma's, or the short ride to the grocery store because a sibling will inevitably cross an imaginary boundary or the child with Asperger's will have his hands all over his sibling, completely ignoring the sibling's personal space. In short, there will be no peace in the vehicle!

Thus, pragmatics are *huge* pieces of the Asperger's puzzle. Think for a moment about the child in the classroom, who talks in that weird, monotone voice, who always seems to be talking loudly to no one in particular, and interrupts constantly to talk (off topic) about carnivorous plants!

Colin's day

The following is a glimpse into a day in the life of an 11-year-old boy, Colin, who has Asperger's syndrome. The pragmatic speech elements of Colin's day will be identified.

6:00am   Colin wakes up, uses the bathroom and starts to get dressed.

6:05am   Colin bounds into his parents' room without knocking (*difficulty generalizing process*; only remembers to knock if it is night time and dark outside). Colin proceeds to go over to his mom, and speaking very loudly (*voice modulation*) in his monotone voice (*prosody*), asks her, "Mother, has my gray polo shirt been laundered recently? Or should I select a different shirt?" (*pedantic*).

6:15am   Colin gets dressed and goes downstairs.

6:30am   Colin's mom asks him if he wants cereal or waffles for breakfast. Colin responds by *perseverating* (to continue a particular thought pattern regarding a specific topic without the ability to shift easily to another topic) on the gray shirt. Mom asks Colin again; this time Colin, who now is on the other side of the room with his back turned toward his mom, responds by screaming, "Waaaaffles!" (*gaze avert, physical proximity, voice modulation*).

7:00am   Dad asks Colin and his older brother, Brad, if either of them want a ride to school today. Brad immediately says "Sure!", while Colin doesn't respond at all (*not reciprocal*). Dad and Brad start talking about Brad's camping trip this weekend with his scout troop. Colin *interrupts* Brad mid-sentence and says: "The cafeteria is serving pizza for lunch today, so I'm buying" (*off topic*). Brad rolls his eyes, sighs loudly and looks exasperated. Colin continues: "I will only buy on days when the cafeteria serves pizza or chicken nuggets. Today I'm buying because pizza is being served" (*not taking turns, not reading facial clues and body language, off topic*).

7:45am   Dad drops Colin and Brad off at school. A classmate, Jake, greets Colin with a head nod and a "Hi, Colin." Colin softly says, "Hi, Jake" after he is about ten feet past Jake (*proximity, gaze avert, voice modulation*).

8:00am   The bell rings and Colin heads off to his classroom. Colin stands in front of his locker, slowly taking things out of his knapsack and getting a stack of books ready for morning classes. Colin appears to be completely unaware that he is blocking the locker next to him, even though the locker's owner is standing next to Colin, saying, "Ahem, excuse me, ahem" while he taps his locker and swings Colin's locker door back and forth (*not responding to body language or verbal clues*).

8:15am   Colin sits at his desk in homeroom, staring out the window (*normal 11-year-old behavior!*). Jake and Nasean are chatting quietly about the most recent action/adventure movie that they both want to see. Nasean asks Colin if he has seen the movie yet. Colin replies, "No, but I'm going to test for my red belt in karate in six months" (*not responding appropriately to content of conversation*).

9:30am   Colin sits in science class, listening to Mr. Zurich explain friction. After a few minutes, Mr. Zurich asks, "Who wants to see the rubber hit the road?" Colin is stymied and looks out the window toward the road (*literal interpretation*).

11:05am   Colin, Ashly, Henry, and Rajay get together, as instructed, to work cooperatively on their Global Studies project. Colin forgot his portion of notes and drawings in his locker (*executive functioning*). Henry, Ashly, and Rajay stand around Henry's desk, looking at Rajay's sketch of the diorama the group will make. Ms. Clifton walks by and asks Colin (who is standing about five feet from his group), "Did your group banish you to the cheap seats?" Ms. Clifton realizes that Colin just doesn't "get it" (*use of idiom/physical proximity*) and rephrases more literally, "Does your group want you to stand that far back?" Colin then walks over to Rajay and stands practically right on top of him (*physical proximity*). Rajay shoots Colin a "look." When Colin does not move away (*difficulty interpreting body language*), Rajay, exasperated, gives Colin a gentle shove and says, "Give me some space, dude." Colin is bewildered. Ashly rolls her eyes and asks, "Let's just move along. This diorama could actually be really cool."

12:15pm   Colin lurches through the lunch line with the rest of the 7th grade, bumping into the person in front of him two different times (*physical proximity*). The server recognizes Colin and makes sure that his fruit does not touch his pizza—she's never seen a 7th grader get so upset about food touching!

12:30pm   Colin finishes lunch and goes outside with the rest of the students. Colin loves to play football with the other boys. In fact, he fancies himself quite the "star" of the lunchtime games (*egocentrism*). Colin is very tall for his age and brings his football to school every day. The others boys laugh at Colin's antics right in front of him, but Colin never seems to get angry (*difficulty interpreting body language, literal interpretation—without regard to tone or inflection in others*). Today, Colin ran (slowly) after the boy he was supposed to block, then attempted to block (threw himself at) another player. Colin missed the player by a mile! However, Colin got up and said, "Did you guys see that, I was about two microns from flattening him like a pancake!" (*pedantic language*). Jared could not contain himself and replied, condescendingly, "Oh yeah, Colin, you're practically ready for the Super Bowl." Colin just beamed from ear to ear (*doesn't understand sarcasm*).

1:00pm   Colin is in study hall. He knows he has homework in math, but can't remember what page. Maybe he left his agenda in his locker? Wait, he forgot to write the homework down in his agenda (*executive function problems*). The teacher and Chenoa are discussing Chenoa's science homework. Colin goes right over and stands between the teacher and Chenoa and asks if he can go to talk to his math teacher (*interrupting/physical proximity*).

4:00pm   Brad and two of his friends come home to find Colin playing his favorite PlayStation 2 video game and eating a bowl of applesauce (fresh apples are too crunchy). One of Brad's friends asks if he can play for a while with Colin. Without looking up, Colin nods yes (*could be the response of a typical boy playing a video game, or gaze avert*). Colin beats Brad's friend, and is able to give the friend helpful tips about the game. After they are out of earshot, the friend asks Brad why Colin doesn't have any friends over after school. Brad replies, "I guess because he doesn't have any real friends."

Chapter 7

Ellie and Dylan:
Ten Years Later

Introduction

In our first book, *Unlocking the Mysteries of Sensory Dysfunction*, we felt it was important to share our personal stories of having a child with sensory dysfunction. At the time we wrote these stories, Ellie and Dylan were five years old and their sensory issues were at the core of our concerns, our routines, and our decisions to seek further evaluation. In sharing their stories we hoped to reach out to other parents and reassure them that they were not alone in facing some of the unique challenges of parenting a child with sensory issues.

As our children have grown, our understanding of their sensory issues has evolved. We wish to continue to share Ellie and Dylan's stories. It continues to fascinate us how they have grown to understand and cope with their individual sensory issues. It is this self-awareness of their sensory issues that has, without a doubt, been the critical element in establishing their independence and self-determination.

The past ten years have been full of surprises for all of us. Here's a glimpse into where we have been and where we are now.

Ellie's story (part one)

Following an uneventful pregnancy and delivery I was thrilled with the arrival of my second daughter Ellie. It was a hot August and I envisioned picnics in the park and walks with the double stroller. Yet, I sensed almost immediately that there was something different about Ellie.

At Ellie's two-month check-up her pediatrician asked me how everything was going. I didn't realize how much I was struggling until I found myself sobbing, "She cries all the time and never sleeps. She gets so frantic in the car seat that she scratches her face until it bleeds. She screams in the front carrier and in the stroller. She doesn't nurse well and takes an hour to drink a bottle." Without realizing it, I had already begun searching for answers. With the best intentions, my pediatrician proceeded to remind me that some babies are fussier than others and to simply be patient. I knew I wouldn't find an answer that day.

I began reading every parenting book I could get my hands on and cornered unsuspecting mothers at the playground. Willing to try anything, I sought advice from family and friends. But, as I confided in a friend when Ellie was a few months old, "No matter what I do, I can't comfort her. I worry that I will never have quality time with her older sister, Lindy, again. I can't get a break because I can't leave her with a sitter. My husband doesn't understand how I feel and thinks it's just an extended post-partum depression." It was as if someone had turned my world upside-down. Suddenly I found myself living in a house of needy people and I had nothing left to give.

So I focused on Ellie's next developmental step to provide that elusive turning point in our lives...maybe when she can crawl, maybe when she can feed herself...maybe when she can walk...Yet, instead of a clear turn in the road there were only rolling hills and deep valleys.

I knew from my first daughter that toddlers are unpredictable, but nothing prepared me for Ellie's intense mood swings...happy one minute, huddled in a corner and hysterical the next. I lived on the edge, never knowing when something would set her off. Usually I did not even know what that something was. As a family we began to tread lightly around Ellie knowing instinctively how weak the structure supporting her world was. Everything was a battle: washing and combing her hair, brushing her teeth, getting dressed, eating a meal, sharing a toy. Unlike her sister, who had shown typical defiance, Ellie's refusals to cooperate were desperate attempts at *avoidance* and completely devoid of reason. Not knowing what else to do, I punished Ellie. She cried and I cried. These were not tears of anger or hurt, but tears of sorrow. Ellie could not tell me what was wrong and I could not help her. A chasm was developing across which neither of us could reach. Having tried everything else, I stopped trying to "fix" Ellie's life or to mold her into the child I wanted her to be. In place of power struggles and tension, I gave her my love unconditionally. I knew how desperately she needed this; little did I know how much she deserved it.

At this time my third daughter, Julia, was born and in the increasingly loud, hectic nature of our household, Ellie sunk into a state of despair. While everyone played games at her older sister's birthday party, Ellie would sob on my shoulder. When friends came over to play, Ellie wandered around confused as if she did not know where to focus her attention. If the baby cried, Ellie covered her ears and hid. The lukewarm bath water felt burning hot; she couldn't tolerate the tags in her clothing; fell out of chairs; ran into furniture; spilled juice getting the cup to her mouth and was terrified when the car turned the corner. Deep down I knew that not only would I have trouble finding answers, but that when I did, they would be far from simple.

The birth of my son Carter, coupled with Ellie beginning preschool, finally gave me the means of comparison to validate years of concern. While I was continually reassured that Ellie was the easiest child in the class, I had only to sit and observe in the classroom to see that Ellie was indeed very different from the other children. Not only were there subtle developmental delays, but there was an immaturity, an inability to prioritize stimuli, and a difficulty processing language. It was at this point that I stopped asking questions and began demanding answers.

By contacting the director of Special Education in my school district, I was able to schedule a series of evaluations for Ellie. While fine motor and speech delays were obvious leads during these evaluations the real answer I had been looking for came with a call from New Hampshire. A friend had heard about the trouble I was having with Ellie and wondered if she could ask me a few questions. After an hour on the phone, I stood in disbelief when this sensory integration specialist said, "Liz, I think she's one of my kids." Here was a woman who could accurately describe Ellie's behavior without ever having met her.

With this friend's guidance, I was able to locate an occupational therapist in my area, who is also trained in sensory integration. The success of Ellie's therapy has changed our lives.

How often I have wished I could go back in time and re-live those early years with Ellie. If only I had known that her behavior was not the result of stubbornness, but a sensory integration problem over which she had no control. Those early years were a tough time not only for Ellie and me, but for our family. For her siblings, it was a time of uncertainty.

We have also come to accept Ellie, as we have all children, for what makes them special, not how well they fit into our mold. As a couple, Richard and I were forced to accept the death of a dream—a dream that we would have four perfect children who would simply glide through life. But, both of us have also been liberated from the confines of this very dream. For no child is perfect and no child escapes life's struggles. As a family we have been dragged unwillingly into the world of special education. However, it has also expanded our horizons in a way we never knew was even possible.

(Adapted from *Unlocking the Mysteries of Sensory Dysfunction* by E. Anderson and P. Emmons. Future Horizons Inc., 1996. Reproduced with permission.)

Ellie's story (part two)

Time after time, I sat down to write this continuation of Ellie's story and yet the words just wouldn't come to me. Then I realized why…in my attempt to simplify and condense almost ten years of her life, I was trying too hard to compartmentalize it. Then I began to realize that neither Ellie nor any child should ever be described using the nature of their special needs as a basis.

I remember Ellie so well at three years old receiving her initial evaluations. I was watching through a one-way mirror at a diagnostic clinic when I heard the psychologist ask, "Ellie, are you a boy or a girl?" Ellie just stared at her blankly. So, she repeated, "Ellie, are you a boy or a girl?" Still no response. So the psychologist tried again, "Ellie, are you a boy or a girl?" Finally, Ellie looked at her and said, "I Ellie." So, when I am asked to describe Ellie as a teenager with a history of behaviors consistent with sensory integration dysfunction, PDD-NOS, ADHD, and a mood disorder, my first response is to say, "Really, she's Ellie."

It was when my fourth child, Carter, was born, and Ellie reached preschool age that I began to develop the means of comparison to validate years of concern. While I was continually reassured that Ellie was one of the easiest children in the class, I had only to observe in the classroom to see that Ellie was indeed different from the other children. At that point, when I looked at Ellie I saw a child with mild to moderate developmental delays with "something else." During those early years, with the help of professionals, we started teasing out what that "something else" was. There was no doubt in anyone's mind that Ellie's delays, attention difficulties, and "odd" behaviors were based in a sensory integration dysfunction. Sharing my experiences as the mother of a child with sensory dysfunction in *Unlocking the Mysteries of Sensory Dysfunction* absolutely changed my life. I am a firm believer that it is in sharing that you truly receive. The years I have spent in the role of parent and teacher working with families, schools, agencies, and parent groups have defined, and continue to define, who I am and what I am all about. The other day I was driving in the car with Ellie and thinking about some of our toughest times and some of our happiest times and I felt a deep sense of awe, because I knew that I was given this child to guide me, to challenge me, to broaden my thoughts, to encourage me to reach out to others, to learn, and to keep me centered on my path. If it were not for Ellie, I wouldn't be who I am today, and I am beginning to realize that if it weren't for me Ellie would not be who she is...and this has taught me to marvel at the interconnectedness we all share in this life.

Certainly over the past ten years, Ellie and our family have experienced some very challenging times as a result of Ellie's sensory, developmental, attention, and social/emotional needs. Anyone who knows me, knows that I don't gloss things over and try to stay based in what is "real." Ellie has had meltdowns in the middle of stores, broken favorite things, run away, physically hurt family members, struggled in school, and had difficulty with peer relationships. But she has also shopped for hours for a special gift, created beautiful works of art for others, and shown the ability to be warm and responsive, made the middle school honor roll and made a good friend. These are the complexities of Ellie and her unique needs. Certainly one of our biggest challenges was nine long months spent on a waiting list for a psychiatric evaluation and services.

As Ellie's needs have changed, so have our ways of supporting them. Ellie no longer receives occupational therapy, speech therapy, or physical therapy, or the services of a paraprofessional who for several years helped her keep focused and stay organized, and helped with curricular and test modifications. She does continue to receive services from a consultant special education teacher as needed and receives counseling and medication monitoring through a Child and Adolescent Health Center. This is not to say that it is not sometimes a bumpy ride...lost books, going to the wrong class, missing the bus, getting lost, forgetting homework, not writing down assignments, sensory overload. And there have been times when I still feel it is necessary to step in and ensure that Ellie's individual needs were being recognized and met.

However, over the years, Ellie's behaviors in our home did become increasingly more challenging. To be honest, I guess they always have been pretty challenging. It's just in the early years I figured all kids her age (especially those with her sensory needs) had equally challenging behaviors. Back then, I focused almost exclusively on Ellie's developmental delays. Perhaps it was just easier and safer in some ways…a fine motor delay?…we knew what to do; a speech delay?…we knew what to do; a gross motor delay?…we knew what to do; learning difficulties?…we knew what to do. But a daughter who was manic, then depressed, anxious, agitated, perseverative, aggressive…I had no idea what to do. So, now I am learning and reading and reflecting and taking each day as it comes. My frustration lies in the fact that Ellie's needs were not simply "developmental delays" (that she would grow out of) or exclusively sensory integration dysfunction. The irony here is that her sensory dysfunction has improved dramatically and really has become a much smaller piece. However, now I feel in many ways like I am back at square one…partnering with the school, nurturing peer relationships, and taking a different approach to the behavior piece. Right now we are in a good place. Ellie is stable, doing well at school, has a couple of new friends, and is involved in several activities. She's happy and that is the most important thing to me.

Liz

Dylan's story (part one)

After a trying pregnancy and a difficult delivery, Dylan was born to two elated, yet weary, parents. Right from the beginning, however, Dylan found touch aversive. He wanted Mom or Dad to be within sight, but did not wish to be cuddled. Dylan was constantly wakeful, taking only 20 minute "power" naps throughout the day and night. It was not until sometime later that I realized only 100 percent cotton clothing and NO blanket would result in his sleeping for longer than five minutes. Strangely, Dylan never became agitated when he was physically cold; he enjoyed it. For example, baths were lukewarm at best, otherwise, he would scream as though he were boiling in oil. Similarly, if his bottle or food were even warm, they would be rejected.

Throughout Dylan's infancy, I thought of myself as a first-time parent struggling with a "difficult" baby, or that was what I was told time and time again by the people I was looking to for advice. Yet, even with these reassurances, I knew in my heart that the truth was not that simple.

When Dylan reached the toddler years his odd behaviors became even more pronounced. No longer was he just "quirky." A strong feeling that something was really wrong began to gnaw at me daily as I witnessed Dylan's sensory problems amplify. While Dylan continued to demand cold food, cold baths and cold sleeping conditions, now anything with even a remotely crunchy texture would also be rejected. In addition, washing Dylan's hair was akin to a world class wrestling event. Because it was such an ordeal, my husband flatly refused to bathe Dylan, and even avoided feeding him. I was appalled to realize that I no longer served hot meals! Dylan's sensory integration disorder had come to rule our lives, and we had never even heard of the term.

Unlike many other children with sensory integration disorder, Dylan reached most of his developmental milestones early. He crawled, sat with a straight back and cruised, all on the day he turned seven months. By nine months Dylan was chasing the dog around the house at break neck speed. When he was 17 months old, his sister Laura was born. While I was in the hospital, Grandma cared for Dylan and remarked, "He is so bright—he knows all his colors and shapes, and can recite the alphabet. He even tells me what he or the dog wants to eat for lunch. But he does act strangely for a 17-month-old."

When the new baby got into a routine, I began to compare her behaviors to Dylan's at the same age, and grew increasingly alarmed. By the time Dylan was two and a half, I began actively seeking help. I was not sure exactly what was wrong, but I knew that some form of intervention was needed. The first two or three "professional" sources I sought out were less than helpful. The tacit inference was that I wanted a perfect child and was therefore looking for something to be wrong. My break finally came when a non-judgmental neighbor suggested that if I had concerns regarding a preschool child, I should contact the local Early Childhood Direction Center. I did just that the next day and was relieved to have an informed and sympathetic ear. I was instructed to phone a local agency, and speak with someone about having Dylan evaluated by a developmental specialist and an occupational therapist. Appointments for the evaluations were set up, and much to my surprise, they were performed at no cost to me.

At age three, Dylan began receiving occupational and physical therapy several times a week as a direct result of the evaluations he had undergone. As a preschooler, his sensory integration problems had become more defined and easier to pinpoint. It was also at this time that Dylan became one of the luckiest children in the world of therapy. His occupational therapist, Eileen, thought he was special. She loved him, and in turn Dylan absolutely adored her.

It was Eileen who assured me that I was not crazy when I described Dylan as being wired differently. In fact, I was shocked when Eileen would ask very pointed questions about Dylan's behaviors and then respond, "That's what I thought you would say." She knew that even though Dylan hated to be touched, loathed swings, and practically went unconscious when asked to ride a see-saw, he would seek out certain sensations in an almost obsessive way. This is a child who would not drink carbonated beverages, eat crunchy cookies, or consume a hot meal. Yet, the longer and faster the slide, the better. He loved the feel of the porcelain tub and actually asked to sleep there. But, this same child reacted to the rubber, textured bath mat in this tub as if it were a bed of thorns.

Dylan has waded out into the Atlantic Ocean with open blisters on his feet and not "noticed" whether his feet hurt or not. However, after his father placed bandages over these blisters, Dylan screamed hysterically for ten minutes, and a stranger from a neighboring cottage came over to ask if we needed help. At this point we removed the bandages and Dylan stopped screaming. Just as he has a "different" awareness of pain, Dylan acts as though his legs are detached. During baths, he will frequently ask, "Mommy, have my legs been washed yet?" to which I reply, "Honey, I just soaped them up and rinsed your legs—all done!"

One of my favorite sensory integration stories about Dylan occurred when he was five years old. Dylan, Laura and I were at the local YMCA signing up for a class when things started getting out of hand and I asked them to please put their coats on NOW (before we were asked to leave)! A couple of minutes later I looked up from my paper work to see and hear a small crowd gathered around a child having a very loud tantrum. At that moment I realized that it was my son! I calmly walked over amidst the glares and asked Dylan what was wrong. He replied through the sobs, "Mommy, you told me to put on my coat, but I can't find it anywhere." It was at this point that I said to Dylan, "Look on your back, you're already wearing your coat." Dylan looked at his arms, saw his coat and replied, "Oh, I'm glad it's not lost!" and promptly stopped crying.

Dylan has worked very hard to overcome his sensory integration problems and has come a long way as a result of this hard work. Our family has also struggled. I think that we all realize now that our life will never be completely "normal," and that's okay. As a family we have made many sacrifices, but we have also made many gains. As a result of living with this disorder, Dylan and his sister Laura have developed great empathy for all people. They bring this compassion into every aspect of their lives. My husband and I have navigated through storm after storm and have not lost sight of the truth—that we have two wonderful kids and not everyone needs a hot meal.

(Adapted from *Unlocking the Mysteries of Sensory Dysfunction* by E. Anderson and P. Emmons. Future Horizons Inc., 1996. Reproduced with permission.)

Dylan's story (part two)

Dylan was diagnosed with Asperger's syndrome at the age of six, after three other comprehensive evaluations had concluded that Dylan was most likely ADHD with some motor delays and a few "quirky" behaviors. Dylan has grown into a handsome teenager who is still active and "quirky," but who is also well liked and hard working. Here is a little "snippet" from events that transpired a few summers ago.

"Ordinary for a day"

"Mom, why can't I be normal? I pray every night that God will make me ordinary for just one day. Then I would be able to figure it out."

I'm too weary for this question at the end of a sultry August day. I only want to get home and sit in front of a fan.

"Figure what out, Dylan?"

"You know, Mom, how to be like the regular kids at camp. I mean, I know I have autism, but I'm a lot more like the regular kids than I am the autistic kids. If I could be ordinary for a day, I would learn all the strategies for getting a friend and I would write them down so I wouldn't forget when I returned to being autistic the next day. Maybe God is waiting until next year when I'm twelve."

Then, in characteristic style, Dylan jumps into the car, takes his action figures out of his backpack and begins to repeat, verbatim, scenes from the 1960s Batman series. As I drive, I reflect on the conundrum that sits next to me. Here is a child who could speak in full sentences, knew all of his shapes, colors, and animal sounds by the age of 17 months, and yet cannot navigate the social world enough to develop or maintain a friendship.

I break from my stunned silence, attempting to reenter the conversation. "Dylan, you have friends at school and camp."

"Mom, did you know that the Siberian tiger is the largest member of the cat family and is the only big cat that is indigenous to North America?"

I learned a long time ago that poor conversational skills, topic perseveration, and inappropriate responses are hallmarks of the mild form of autism that Dylan has, called Asperger's syndrome. I very pointedly bring Dylan back to the original topic: "I said I thought you had friends at school and camp."

Dylan, eyes downcast, still playing with the Batman action figure, responds very matter of factly, "I don't have anybody who fits the definition of a REAL friend."

"Well, what's the definition of a real friend?" I ask.

At this point, I was fully expecting a dictionary definition of the word "friend." Instead, Dylan said, in his characteristically monotone voice, "Mom, friends are people who want to be with you, even when they don't have to. Friends call each other up on the phone, friends invite you over to play at their house, and friends have sleepovers and birthday parties. Nobody has ever invited me to a sleepover. Nobody ever wants to come to my house even though I ask them all the time."

Now it's my turn to change the subject in midstream, "Hey, what do you say we go to McDonald's and get a little treat before we pick your sister up from her camp?" The truth is that the lump in my throat is so big, that if I allow myself to start crying now, I will be unable to drive.

As I pull into those Golden Arches, my mind starts to call up vivid images and vignettes of Dylan's early childhood. I can see the cherubic baby who screamed when swaddled, never slept for more than 20 minutes at a time, and who refused to eat warm foods. I remember with horror the loquacious toddler who howled and tantrumed when we went to the park because he hated the swings, merry-go-round and sandbox so much. I recall the discriminating (ultra picky) eater, who would refuse a piece of pizza shaped like a triangle, but would eat the same slice if it were cut into squares. How could I forget the fascination with construction equipment, which eventually faded into an obsession with Batman, which was, over time, eclipsed by a need to learn, talk, think, and read about the Japanese language and the origin of Ninjas? Presently, his area of intense interest is writing and reading action/adventure stories and poetry.

My reminiscence is interrupted by an angry wail, "Stupid, stupid seatbelt! I can never unbuckle it—I'll never be able to unbuckle it…"

As I lean over to assist him, Dylan looks plaintively at me and says, "Do you remember when I was four years old and I asked you what did I do wrong when I was in your uterus to make me so different?"

"Vaguely," I lie (the whole conversation was permanently etched in my psyche). "What made you think of that right now?"

"Can I have a double cheeseburger meal, I'm really hungry."

"No, this is just a snack, and why did you ask about when you were four?"

Just as we approach the counter, Dylan growls, "You never let me have the double cheeseburger meal. You said I could have a treat."

Dylan is rapidly beginning to "meltdown," so I usher him out of the queue and begin to speak to this tall eleven-year-old, who has the vocabulary of an adult, and the emotional development of a five-year-old. Dylan needs prompting to lower his voice, look at me, and not become completely distraught because he is not getting a double cheeseburger meal.

The good news is that I have learned to hone in on the problem rapidly: it is usually the wording. "What exactly is bothering you? I said we were stopping for a little treat."

Dylan responds without missing a beat, "That's exactly it, first you said 'treat,' then you changed it to 'snack.' A treat is something special that you don't get very often. A snack means a small amount of food."

This is a prime example of the way children with Asperger's interpret language very literally. I remember the time Dylan came home from 1st grade with different clothes on because he had spilled paint in art class. That night, when I asked him to take off his clothes and get into the tub, he just stood there like a zombie, then started to cry. When I asked him why he was crying instead of taking his clothes off, he said, "These aren't my clothes, these are nurses' office clothes!" From that moment on, I became very conscious of the disparity between Dylan's superficial language skills (adult-like vocabulary, sentence structure, and syntax) and his ability to *comprehend* language. I later learned that abstract concepts like emotions, and subtle conversational cues such as body language and facial expressions are very difficult for children with Asperger's syndrome to interpret.

Thus, I shift to plan B. "Dylan, what I meant was, that you could have either a hamburger or a milkshake, as a snack-sized treat."

"Oh, then I'll have a chocolate shake.

I quickly place our order and we find a table in the middle of the crowded dining area. Dylan happily guzzles his shake while I bite into my burger.

"Gee, Mom, I guess you've abandoned the Weight Watchers' plan, huh?"

Did I mention that children with Asperger's have a real deficit in the social skills arena? I pointed out to Dylan that the comment he just made could be construed as unkind. He was very surprised. "Oh, I didn't mean to hurt your feelings, I was just making an observation. You keep telling me not to just talk about myself all the time. Conversation is so confusing—how does everybody else keep the rules straight?" Dylan's frustration was obvious and heartfelt.

That night, when I tucked the kids into bed, I thought about Dylan's world. The world of a child who has Asperger's syndrome; a child who has always been ruled by his inflexibility and anxiety.

From the ages of three to five, when other kids his age were playing, napping, or watching Mr. Rogers, Dylan was spending Monday through Friday afternoons in the Rehabilitation Department of a local hospital receiving speech therapy, occupational therapy, and physical therapy. When the other kindergartners were playing together and making friends, Dylan was lost in the fray, trying hard to participate in a world he could only partially understand. During early elementary school, he was the "really smart, but weird kid," who needed a paraprofessional to help him keep himself together and navigate the social world. As Dylan grew and became more socially aware, he longed for friendships and a sense of belonging within his peer group. I honestly feel that no child has worked more purposefully or intensively to overcome his deficits than Dylan. He has hung in tenaciously, experiencing one social disaster after another, with successes being few and far between.

Now, Dylan is twelve and attends middle school. If middle school is a social and developmental nightmare for the average child, it is a social black hole for a child with autism. Dylan knows that, because of his autism, he must work harder than his peers to "maintain" himself and get through the school day. Fortunately, Dylan has persevered so far. He still needs a paraprofessional to help him with the social labyrinth of school, but he is fully included in regular education and takes some advanced academic courses. He has even earned his red belt in karate, learned to play the piano, and is a member of the concert choir.

However, the best news of all came just yesterday. Dylan was invited to his first ever sleepover! When I asked him how he felt about that, he stammered, through tears, "I think this must be what it feels like to be an 'ordinary' kid."

Polly

We recognize that life is dynamic and we don't know where Ellie and Dylan will be ten years from now. But, what we are sure of is that Ellie and Dylan are a couple of great kids who are becoming aware of who they are and are developing the tools they will need to navigate their futures.

In Conclusion

All of us process sensory input 24 hours a day, starting from the moment we are born. It is the integration of this sensory information that shapes our perceptions, defines our realities, and drives our behaviors. We all exist as sensory beings, with our own unique perspectives. We hope that this book promotes a greater awareness and understanding of sensory issues and sensory integration dysfunction. Sensory issues and sensory integration dysfunction touches all of our lives in some way—a child, a student, a family member, a coworker, or a friend who has an autism spectrum disorder, ADHD, a learning disability, or cerebral palsy. It is our opinion that the sensory piece for many children has been overlooked, downplayed, or undervalued for too long. Now is the time to bring sensory dysfunction into the forefront and begin to look at home and school, learning and behavior differently—through a sensory lens.

Sensory Integration Activities

The Tactile System

"Feely box"

Use a plastic container, pillow case or shoe box. Place different objects in the container and have the child reach in and guess what object he or she is touching.

Sensory bin

Fill a large plastic container with rice, pasta, corn meal, popcorn, sand, water, birdseed, etc. and place different objects in it. Have child use hands to sort and sift through to find objects. Try different materials that are warm, cold, bumpy, smooth, etc.

Dress-up clothes

Keep a box of "hand-me-downs" or yard sale dress-up clothes. Look for items that have different textures (silky, furry, feathers, etc.), colors, patterns.

Bathtub play

Encourage your child to use different soaps and sizes and types of towels while in the tub. Offer different soaps, scented, oatmeal soap, shaving cream, lotion soap, animal shapes, foam soap, exfoliating body wash. Offer different types of textures for washing: thick wash cloths, soft, plastic brushes, kitchen sponges, foam pot scrubbers, handi-wipes, loofa sponges, bath mitts, etc.

Toys

Offer the child toys with different textures—squishy, hard, rough, smooth, bumpy, soft, etc.

Make a "hotdog in a bun"

Roll the child up tightly in a blanket.

Cook together

Anything that allows the child to "mix" something "hands-on" such as cookie dough, bread dough, cake batter, pizza dough, spreading toppings.

Fingerpainting activities

Use finger paint and mix in other materials to get a different sensory experience, for example, rice, sand, seeds, popcorn, etc. Or make your "fingerpaint" by using pudding, shaving cream, or Jello on a cookie sheet or tray.

Foods

Encourage the child to try new foods with different tastes and textures.

The Vestibular System

Hippity-hopping

A Hippity Hop is a large ball with a handle that child sits on and hops and bounces. Try it on grass and carpet.

Rolling

Roll down a grassy hill.

Swinging

Playground swings, tire swings, rope swings, monkey swings, "trapeze," "rings."

Swinging in a blanket

Have child lie down on a large blanket. Have two adults hold opposite corners of the blanket, pick up child in blanket slightly off the floor or ground and swing.

Sliding

Playground slides, swimming pool slides, sledding.

Obstacle course

Set up an obstacle course at home (inside or outside) that encourages crawling, climbing, jumping, balancing, etc.

Riding vehicles

Tricycles, bicycles, scooters, Kettle cars, big wheel, child-size motorized vehicles.

Running/jogging

Game of tag, foot races, kickball, T-ball, soccer, different kinds of ball games.

Jumping

From a high place to a lower place (bottom stair), jumping in place, jump rope, standing broad jump, running broad jump, trampoline, jumping jacks, hop scotch, jumping in a pile of leaves.

Spinning

Supervision required—these activities may result in intense sensory input… merry-go-round, sit 'n' spin, twirling.

The Proprioceptive System

Carry heavy things

Laundry basket, grocery bag, gallon of milk, container of laundry detergent.

Pushing activities

Strollers, child-size grocery cart, toy lawn mower, toddler push toys, carry knapsack filled with toys, etc.

Pulling activities

Wagons, tug-of-war, toddler pull toys.

"Crashing" activities

Set up couch cushions, pillows, comforters, and allow child to jump into them, Velcro walls, bumper cars.

Crab walk

Wheelbarrow walk

Pouring
Allow the child to pour from different size and shape containers into another
container. For example: water, sand, rice, pasta, seeds, popcorn, etc.

Spreading activities
Allow child to spread his or her own peanut butter, jelly, fluff, cream cheese.

Hanging activities
With close adult supervision and/or support, have the child use the monkey bars
at the playground.

"Push place"
Designate a spot in your house or classroom where the child can push with hands
or feet against a wall.

Batting/swinging activities
Baseball, golf, tennis, racquet ball, etc.

Appendix 2

Treatment Options

The following options are currently being utilized for the treatment of sensory dysfunction. Our belief is that it is up to parents to become the "ultimate consumer"—reading, asking questions, and making informed decisions about any form of intervention that their child may receive. We also strongly recommend that any treatment option you wish to explore be discussed with and supervised by the appropriate professional(s).

Allergies
There are many different treatment options available for the environmental, food, and chemical sensitivities that some believe are associated with sensory dysfunction. Some of these include dietary changes, food elimination, modifications to the physical environment, or desensitization protocols.

Auditory integration training
Originally developed by a French physician, Dr. Berard, this treatment option makes use of different sound frequencies to exercise the ear in order to desensitize and improve hearing and communication skills.

Behavior modification
There are many different forms of behavior modification paradigms. These methods typically break behaviors down into component parts and apply specific structured techniques to modify, change, or shape those behaviors.

"Brushing protocol"
A "brushing" program which utilizes a "surgical" brush to "brush" an individual's arms, hands, back, legs, and feet in an attempt to help the individual process and

organize sensory information. This "brushing" is followed by joint compressions where each joint is supported as pressure is applied to it. This treatment approach was developed by an occupational therapist, Patricia Wilbarger.

Homeopathy
Promotes the use of natural ingredients and organic materials to treat illnesses to attain or maintain good health and development.

Oral tactile stimulation
In this option, a finger, wrapped in a wash cloth, or a "Nuk" massager is used to swipe across the roof of an individual's mouth from side to side three times quickly, then exiting the mouth. This treatment option is used before and during each meal as is tolerated. It is designed to stimulate the mouth for increased awareness/decreased awareness of oral sensory stimulation.

Osteopathy
Centers around physical manipulation of the body and the use of natural and homeopathic remedies to attain or maintain good health and development and/or treat illness (e.g., chiropractic).

Sensory integration therapy
The goal of sensory integration therapy is to facilitate the development of the nervous system's ability to process sensory input in a more "normal" way through addressing the vestibular, proprioceptive, and tactile systems.

Appendix 3

Resources

American Psychiatric Association (2000) *Diagnostic and Statistical Manual of Mental Disorders, Fourth Edition.* Washington, DC: American Psychiatric Association.

Anderson, E. and Emmons, P. (1996) *Unlocking the Mysteries of Sensory Dysfunction.* Arlington, TX: Future Horizons Inc.

Ayres, A.J. (1979) *Sensory Integration and the Child.* Los Angeles: Western Psychological Services.

Frith, U. (1991) "Asperger and his Syndrome." In U. Frith (ed) *Autism and Asperger Syndrome.* Cambridge: Cambridge University Press.

Heward, W. (1996) *Exceptional Children.* Upper Saddle River: Prentice Hall Inc.

Learning Disabilities Association of America (2005) "Learning Disabilities: Signs, Symptoms and Strategies." Pittsburgh, PA: Learning Disabilities Association of America. www.ldanatl.org/aboutld/parents/ld_basics/index.asp

Siegel, B. (1996) *The World of the Autistic Child: Understanding and Treating Autistic Spectrum Disorders.* New York: Oxford University Press.

University of the State of New York—The State Education Dept Office of Vocational and Educational Services (2004) *Individual Evaluation and Eligibility Determinations for Students with Disabilities.* Albany, NY: New York State Department of Education.

Index

academic achievement,
    difficulties 32, 34
activities, sensory
    integration 123, 165–68
activity levels, high/low 32–3,
    97–8
adaptive equipment 124
adaptive skills development 51,
    52–3
aggression 97, 99
allergies 169
arena style evaluation 63
aromas 124, 125
Asperger's syndrome 10, 68, 69,
    71–2, 130–50
    case study 131–7, 147–50,
        154–7
    diagnosis 130–8
    example of a daily
        routine 147–50
    language deficits of 137,
        138–47
    school and 96
    social interaction
        difficulties 71, 131–7,
        138–50, 155–7
    symptoms 131–8
assessment and
    evaluation 29–31, 55–64
    formal 63
    gathering/documenting
        information 56–9
    individual 63, 65–6
    informal 63–4
    programs and
        services 64–6
    psychological 61
    role of 60–1
    and symptom
        pervasiveness 55–6
    terminology 61–4
attention deficit disorder
    (ADD) 73

attention deficit hyperactivity
    disorder (ADHD) 9, 10, 68
    case study 154–7
    combined type 73
    definition 73–4
    hyperactive-impulsive
        type 73
    inattentive type 73
attention-seeking behaviors 117
audiology assessments 62
auditory defensiveness 36–40
auditory dysfunction 36–40, 80,
    114–15, 120
auditory integration training 169
autism spectrum disorders 9, 68
    definition 69–72
    visual schedules for 83–4
    see also specific disorders
autistic disorder 17, 69–71
    atypical autism 71
awareness of sensory
    needs 124–5
Ayres, J.A. 9, 14–16, 34

babies 64
    adaptive skills
        development 53
    communication
        difficulties 51
    developmental
        milestones 21–3
    signs of sensory
        dysfunction 41–3
balance problems 35–6
bathing/showering 127–8, 165
bedtimes 129
behavior modification 169
behavioral management
    strategies 118–22
    helpful 118–20
    preventative 122
    unhelpful 121–2
Berard, Dr. 169
bipolar disorder 74
blocking/containing,
    physical 122
body language 143, 148–9
"brushing protocol" 169–70

case studies 10, 18, 36–41
    Asperger's
        syndrome 131–7,
        147–50, 154–7
    Dylan 10, 56–7, 151,
        156–63
    elementary school
        children 86, 90–3
    Ellie 10, 151–6, 163
    middle/high school
        children 86, 93–7
    preschoolers 86–90
central auditory processing
    disorder 10, 72
central nervous system 15–16
    plasticity 16
challenging behaviors 32, 34
    management techniques
        for 116–22
    as means of
        communication 97–9
    misunderstanding 117–18
    and teaching
        modifications 112, 114
childhood disintegrative
    disorder 69
co-conditions
    (co-morbidity/concomitant
    diagnoses) 55, 67–75
cognitive development
    problems 51–3
color 123–4
communication difficulties 51–2
    of autistic disorder 70
    in babies 42–3, 51
    managing children
        with 116–17
    recording 103
    in toddlers 45–6, 52
cooking 166
coordination 19–20
    difficulties 17, 32, 33,
        35–6
cravings, sensory 82
criterion-referenced tests 63
curricular adaptations 106,
    111–15

daily routines 36–40
defining sensory
    dysfunction 32–66
development 20–8, 29–31,
    41–50
developmental screenings 65
diagnosis 59
        Asperger's syndrome 130–8
discriminatory touch 38
displeasure, expression of 121
distractibility 97, 98
"do as I do" 119
dreamers 114, 115
dressing 128, 165
DSM-IV (*Diagnostic and Statistical
    Manual of Mental Disorders,
    Fourth Edition*) 55, 69, 73,
    130–8
dyscalculia 72
dysgraphia 72
dyslexia 72
dyspraxia 72

early intervention 64–5
egocentrism 149
emotional development 28–9
emotional difficulties 42–3,
    45–6, 54, 134–5, 148
emotional lability 97, 98
environmental
    modifications 122–7
ethnicity 60

facial expressions 83, 143, 148
"feely box" 165
fingerpainting 166
food 129, 166
forms, school 102–8
frustration levels 97, 98

gaze avert 144, 148, 150
generalization difficulties 146–7,
    148
gustatory symptoms 36, 37, 38,
    82

hand pouches 81
headphones, noise-muffling 80
hidden disorders 67

home management
    techniques 116–29
home/school
    partnerships 99–101
homeopathy 170
homework 93–7
honesty, inappropriate 156
hula hoops 81, 83
hyper activity 32–3, 97–8
hypo activity 32–3, 97–8

icons 83–4
"if, then" statements 119
ignoring, planned
    (extinction) 121
intelligence quotient (IQ) 61
interrupting 90, 140–1, 148,
    150

jogging 167
jumping 114, 167

language difficulties 51–2
    in Asperger's 137, 138–47
    delays 32, 33
    evaluation 62
    pedantic language 139–40,
        148, 150
learning disabilities 9, 10, 68,
    72–3, 112
learning style adaptations 106,
    111–15
lesson plans 113–15
lighting 124
literal interpretations 145–6,
    149, 156

management techniques 116–29
    behavioral 118–22
    environmental 122–7
    self-care strategies 127–9
    see also treatment options
medication 75
"meltdowns" 57–8, 156
modeling behavior 119
motor skills 32, 34–6, 54–5, 62,
    104
multidisciplinary teams 63–5
muscles 20, 36
music 124

needs of the child 61
noise 124
non-compliance 97, 98
nonverbal behavior
    impairments 131–2
nonverbal consequences 121–2
norm-referenced tests 63
notebooks 56–9
nurses, school 80

obstacle courses 167
occupational therapy 79
    evaluations 61, 62–3
    in school 85, 86
olfactory dysfunction 39, 82,
    115
oral tactile stimulation 170
osteopathy 170
over-reactive children 17, 32, 33,
    109

paraprofessionals 78–9, 96, 97,
    157
    1:1 paras 79
peer relationships 132–3
perception 19
perseveration 97, 98, 148, 154
pervasive developmental disorder,
    not otherwise specified
    (PDD-NOS) 69, 71
pervasive developmental
    disorders 69
physical education instructors,
    adapted 79
physical proximity issues 97–8,
    147–50
physical therapy 62, 79, 85–6
play, impoverished 136–7
point of view (POV), of the
    child 86, 88, 91, 94–5
"pokers" 114, 115
pragmatics 138–50
preschoolers 26–7
    adaptive skills
        development 53
    communication
        difficulties 52
    preparing children to
        learn 109–10
    in preschool class 86–90

services for 65–6
signs of sensory
dysfunction 46–8
preventative behavioral
strategies 122
programs and services
assessment for 64–6
early intervention 64–5
eligibility for 66
preschool age 65–6
proprioceptive system 19, 20,
36–40
and school life 85, 114,
115
sensory integration activities
for 167–8
prosody, odd 141, 142, 148
psychological evaluations 61
psychologists, school 80
pull-out/push-in therapy 79

rapport between home and
school 99
reciprocity, lack of
social/emotional 134–5, 148
record keeping 56–9
redirection/switching
gears 118–19
reinforcement 105, 119
relaxers 105, 123–4
response prevention 120
restricted interests 70–1, 135–7,
144–5
Rett's disorder 69, 71
riding bikes 167
"righting a wrong" 120
routines 36–40, 123, 126, 129,
136
"runners and hiders" 97, 98
running 167

school 76–115, 116–29
adapting to the
child 101–15
challenging behavior as
means of communication
in 97–9
elementary 86, 90–3
home/school
partnerships 99–101

lesson plans 113–15
middle/high school 86,
93–7, 110–11, 157
parental roles 76
personnel 78–80, 100
preparing children to
learn 109–11
self-monitoring
students 111
sensory dysfunctions
in 80–6
situations and
solutions 80–6
special education 77–8
teacher's role 76, 78,
86–99
teaching/curriculum
modifications 111–15
school forms 102–8
abbreviated secondary
school form 108
basic child information
form 102
classroom management
form 105
communication abilities
form 103
learning style/curricular
adaptations form 106
motor needs/adaptations
form 104
work samples form 107
school-aged children 27–8,
48–50
self-calming behaviors 117–18
self-care strategies 62, 127–9
self-concept, poor 32, 34
self-monitoring, students 111
sensory activities 123, 165–68
sensory approaches 61
sensory
bags/baskets/bins 126–7,
165
sensory cravings 82
sensory defensiveness 17
sensory integration 14–31
adaptive behavior and 16
definition 14
development 20–8, 29–31
drive for 16

history of 14–16
and reality 19
sensory processing 16–19
sensory systems 19–20
sequential, hierarchical
development 16
and social and emotional
development 28–9
sensory integration therapy 170
sensory interpretation 18
sensory modulation 17
sensory needs, awareness
of 124–5
sensory orientation 18
sensory overload 38, 119
sensory processing 16–19
sensory registration 17, 18
sensory response 17, 18
sensory systems 19–20, 34–6
see also proprioceptive
system; tactile system;
vestibular system
services see programs and services
sharing 133–4, 152
"shouters" 114
"shut down" 97, 98
sign language 83
"slow gear" kids 86–90
social difficulties 54
in babies 42–3
interactional 69–70, 71,
131–50, 155–7
in toddlers 45–6
social history 61
social interaction 28–9
in Asperger's syndrome 71,
131–50, 155–7
in autistic disorder 69–70
social misfits 137
social stories 81
social workers, school 79
special education 77–8
speech delays 32, 33
speech evaluation 62
speech therapy 79
stereotyped behaviors 70, 71,
135–7
stimulation, level of 122–3

"stopping behavior before it
    starts" 119–20
student portfolios 101
study guides/outlines 83
symptoms/signs of sensory
    dysfunction 32–4, 51–5
        in babies 41–3
        pervasiveness 55–6
        in preschoolers 46–8
        school-aged child 48–50
        in toddlers 44–6

tactile system 19, 35, 36–40
    school and 80–1, 115
    sensory integration activities
        for 165–66
tactilely defensive children 80–1,
    119
"taking a break" 120, 126
teachers
    analyzing the situation 86,
        88–9, 91–2, 95
    describing behavior 86, 87,
        90–1, 93
    as detectives 86–99
    never forgets factor 86, 88,
        91, 94
    point of view of the
        child 86, 88, 91, 94–5
    pre-behavior situation 86,
        88, 91, 94
    role 76, 78
    special education 77, 78
    strategies 86, 89–90, 92–3,
        95–6
temperament 28
texture 36, 38–40, 81, 124
"time out" 121
toddlers 24–6
    adaptive skills
        development 53
    communication
        difficulties 45–6, 52
    early intervention 64
    signs of sensory
        dysfunction 43–6
toothbrushing 128
topics, staying on 142–3, 148
touch see tactile system

"touchers" 114, 115
toys 81, 165
transitions 105, 124
treatment options 169–70
        see also management
            techniques; medication
turn taking 140, 148

under-reactive children 17, 32,
    33, 86–90, 109

verbal warnings 80
vestibular system 19, 35–41
    and school life 85–6
    sensory integration activities
        for 166–7
visual assessment 62
visual barriers 125
visual cues 125
visual dysfunction 37–9, 82–4,
    114, 115
visual school schedules 83–4
visual supports 125
visual-motor skills 62
voice
    inflection 142
    modulation difficulties 141,
        148
    sing-song 141, 142

"whole child" 60–1
Wilbarger, P. 170